The Comprehensive Guide to Passing the Virginia Real Estate Sales Exam

Table of Contents

The Comprehensive Guide

To

Passing the Virginia Real Estate Sales Exam

Real Estate Review

Classes of Property

Property falls under the term hereditaments. This is any property that can be inherited. Hereditaments fall under personal property or real property. Real property is land and any permanent attachments, such as buildings. Personal property is not attached to the land like real property. Storage bins would be an example of personal property. It is possible for personal property to become real property if it is permanently attached by articles such as bolts, plaster, and screws. The intent of the tenant who adds property will be considered when determining the property's class. For example, a trade fixture that is added solely for the purpose of the tenant remains his property. Tenants must repair any damage caused by trade fixtures.

Land Characteristics

Land includes surface rights, subsurface rights, and air rights. There are both physical and economic characteristics of land.

Physical characteristics:

- **Immobility** – Land is considered immobile because it cannot be moved. Portions of land may be moved, but it cannot be moved entirely.
- **Indestructibility** – Land's indestructibility makes it a worthwhile investment. Weather will cause changes to land, but it cannot be completely destroyed.
- **Non-homogeneity** – Each portion of land is unique, lacking homogeneity. There are identifying characteristics on each portion of land.

Economic characteristics:

- **Scarcity** – Land has limited availability, which makes it scarce, and some areas have more land available than others. Scarcity increases price, which is expected to increase the value of the property over time.
- **Modifications** – Changes to the land or modifications affect the value over time. Modifications to one property will affect the value of neighboring properties. Not all modifications will increase the value of the land.
- **Fixity** of location – Is the physical characteristic of real estate that subjects it to the influence of its surroundings, creating investment permanence. It takes time for land to pay back the initial investment that is made.
- **Situs** – The land's location, or situs, has an effect on its value. The preferences of buyers are the most influential economic characteristic to affect price.

Encumbrances

An encumbrance is anything that harms or blocks property value such as a lien or unpaid taxes. Ownership and property rights are difficult to determine when there is an encumbrance. Types of encumbrances are:

- **Encroachment** – Encroaching is any intrusion onto the surface or in the airspace of land, and it can be caused by poor surveying. Structures that encroach on neighboring properties are examples of encroachments.
- **Easement** – The right to use another person's land for a specific purpose is an easement. A road through one person's property to gain access to another's is an example of an easement. Common easements are:
  - **Easement Appurtenant** – Two properties with two owners may require an appurtenant. The dominant estate benefits from the easement, and the servient estate is the land that has the burden of the easement. For example, the property with the road on it is the servient estate.
  - **Easement in Gross** – Multiple pieces of land that are affected at the same time require easement in gross. Utilities making use of land is an example of easement in gross.
  - **Easement by necessity** – Court ordered easement.
  - **Easement by condemnation** – The government that has exercised its right under eminent domain.
  - **Easement by prescription** – Right is created forcibly.

- **Liens** – A lien is a financial claim on a property or owner that is used to secure a debt. Liens may be voluntary or involuntary, depending on whether or not the owner enters the lien willingly. Mortgages are voluntary liens because the owner enters into the agreement willingly.
  - **Mechanic's lien** – A mechanic's lien is involuntary. It may be initiated by those who have provided labor or materials to improve the property, such as contractors that have not

been paid. There is a statutory period for notice and foreclosure. This lien is given priority over most others.

- o **Foreclosure** – The legal process of selling an owner's property to pay a debt. It may be put on hold by the court once the owner posts a bond to pay the amount owed.
- o **Non-judicial foreclosure** – A foreclosure that occurs when the statutory power of the sale clause in the mortgage allows the lender to sell the property in the event of a default.
- o **Material Man's lien** – Similar to a mechanic's lien, but applies more to the person or company who has supplied the materials.

- **Judgment** – The owner's obligation of payment as determined by the court.
  - o **Writ of attachment** – The order that specifies property to be sold if an owner does not comply with the judgment.
  - o **Writ of execution** – The order given to force a judgment made against an asset such as property. To collect an asset that has been ordered to be turned over.
- **Tax liens** – Available at the federal, state, and local level, tax liens allow the government to collect unpaid taxes by placing a lien on property. This lien has the highest priority and is enforced by the tax sale. A tax deed is given to the purchaser.
  - o **Property tax lien** – Set at the local level, property tax liens are used to cover property taxes, local taxes, or state taxes. It is also called a special assessment tax lien.
  - o **Federal tax lien** – Liens that are placed by the IRS are federal tax liens. They are used to secure the payment of income, gift, and other taxes.
  - o **State tax lien** – Processed at the state level, these liens are used for state income tax, sales tax, etc.

A **cloud on title** refers to any irregularity in the chain of title that would impair a transferor's ability to convey "clear" title to a transferee.

Adverse possession occurs when a person occupies and claims a property as his own. Obtaining a title in Virginia requires 15 continuous years of inhabiting a property.

Types of Ownership

Ownership requires the seller to provide a marketable title, which means that the property is transferable. Any claims from outside parties make the title unacceptable and prevent the transfer of ownership. It is important to carefully investigate titles for any clouds or encumbrances before attempting to transfer property:

- **Title search** – This process is designed to determine if the owner of the property has saleable interest, any restrictions or allowance for a property, or any liens or foreclosures.
- **Chain of title** – Conducting research on the current and past title holders. It shows the history of transfers of title to a property.

- **Grantee index** – An alphabetical list of purchasers of the property.
- **Grantor index** – An alphabetical list of sellers of the property.

Forms of Ownership:

- **Estate in severalty** – Estate in severalty is also called sole ownership. A single property holder or entity owns the title. No other owners or businesses are connected to the property.
- **Tenancy in common** – A form of ownership in which two or more parties possess the property simultaneously. Inheritance is a common cause of tenancy in common as well as a deed or court order.
- **Joint tenancy** – Similar to tenancy in common, joint tenancy involves two or more parties, but it determines the rights of survivorship. Upon the death of one tenant, the interest is given to the surviving tenants. There are four unities in joint tenancy:
    - **Unity of time** – The tenants obtain ownership at the same time; no one may be added later.
    - **Unity of title** – The interest in the title is obtained in the same way as a will.
    - **Unity of interest** – The tenants share interest equally.
    - **Unity of possession** – All tenants have the same right to occupy the property in their interest.
- **Tenancy by the entirety** – In states without community property, such as Virginia, tenancy by the entirety shares equal interest between married individuals. The interest conveys to the surviving spouse at the time of death.

Community property – a form of ownership commonly defined as property owned by spouses – can also be owner through a partnership established by law. Virginia is not a community property state.

- **Partnerships** – Typically used when property is a form of investment, partnerships allow profits and losses to be shared.
    - **General partnership** – Also called a regular partnership, the most common type of partnership. The partners share all debts and liabilities equally.
    - **Limited partnership** – Limited partners share in profits and debts but do not share the full liability. The general partner is still necessary and responsible for the liability and obligations.
- **Corporations** – Entities that have rights to purchase land, transfer property, and create contracts. Corporations pay income taxes that partnerships do not have to pay.
- **Fee simple estate** – The greatest possible ownership of real property is considered the fee simple estate. It provides property owners with the right to rent, sell, occupy, build, demolish, limit access, mine, and extract resources.
- **Insolvent estate** – an estate in which the property owner's debts are greater than the assets. Debts must be paid before heirs can inherit.

Property Descriptions

Deeds require accurate descriptions of property. In order to ensure that real property is described in a manner that is recognizable, different methods are used:

- **Metes and bounds** – This method of description uses the boundaries and shape of the land to describe it. The surveyor moves clockwise to make the description, and permanent monuments are chosen when possible.
- **Rectangular survey system** – Also called the public land survey system, the rectangular system is used to subdivide the land using latitude and longitude.
- **Government or US public land system** –Most commonly used method to survey and spatially identify land or property parcels before designating ownership, whether for sale or transfer.
- **Congressional townships** – A survey method that refers to a square unit of land that is usually six miles on each side. Each township is divided into 36 one-square-mile sections that can be further subdivided for sale.
- **Principal meridians** – Method that uses a principal meridian line used for survey control in a large region, which divides townships between north/south/east/west.
- **Recorded plat** – Also known as the lot and block survey system; this system is used for lots in a variety of areas (i.e. heavily populated metropolitan, suburban, and exurbs). Especially used to plot large areas of a property into smaller lots and land areas
- **Assessor's parcel number (APN)** – Also known as an appraisal's account number, a number assigned to parcels of property by the area's jurisdiction for identification and recordkeeping. The APN is unique within the particular jurisdiction, and may conform to certain formatting standards that hold identifying information, such as the property type or location.

Zoning

Zoning and planning laws were established by the Standard State Zoning Enabling Act and the Standard City Planning Enabling Act, which are published by the US Department of Commerce.

Land use is planned at the national, state, city, and county level. Local governments only have the authority assigned to them by state governments according to Dillon's Rule, but the Home Rule allows the state to transfer authority to local governments.

Planning commissions are established by city councils or county commissions. They study and plan legislative actions and settle quasi-judicial matters. The zoning board handles permits and administrative decision appeals. The board does not handle construction standards, which are found in building codes.

Zoning is used to reduce density and service delivery costs. Its main use is segregating land uses that are not compatible. Impact fees address the changes in a community and are charged on new developments that may have an effect on the community.

Systems:

- **Shoreland zoning** – Zoning rules to protect water quality and the environment around waterways.
- **Floodplain zoning** – Protects the health, property, and lives of people.
- **Euclidean zoning** – Separates land into geographical districts.
- **Effects based planning** – Also called performance zoning, the parameters are flexible and have performance or goal standards for developments.
- **Incentive zoning** – A reward based system that is used to help developments reach goals.
- **Form-based zoning** – Zoning that regulates the forms of land use.
- **Cluster zoning** – Provides zones that allow clustering of properties to create open space.

Rezoning requires legislative action, and most states requires a period for public discussion. There are different reasons for rezoning:

- falling in line with long term plans
- changes that make current zoning use unreasonable
- mistake with the original zoning

Government Rights in Land

The government can draw a fine line as to where it has rights to land and where it doesn't. However, the US government can take private property through the use of eminent domain or expropriation.

Escheat – A common law that means to fall back, escheat is applied when a landowner dies with no heirs or instructions for the property. In this case, the land falls back to the ownership of the government.

Property taxes – Property taxes are collected on the state, city, and county level. The most common is an *ad valorem* tax which is created specifically based on the monetary value of the property. It is usually created at the time of purchase of the property although it can also be done on an annual basis.

Gains and Losses

A capital gain is realized when the property is sold and the sale price is more than the purchase price. Many jurisdictions impose a capital gains tax and require several forms of documentation to ensure accurate transactions.

Depreciation generally refers to the decrease in value over time. This can occur due to unfavorable home modifications, damages, or changes in property costs and prices.

Estates

"Estate" generally refers to a person's property, entitlements or assets, but is also applied to a large parcel of land that includes the real and personal property. It is usually defined as the houses and grounds of a very large property, including woodlands, farmlands, gardens, and landscapes. Estates are generally owned by individuals or jointly, or through title by contract.

- **Freehold estate** – an estate that has the exclusive right to possession and use of the property for an indefinite amount of time.
  Fee simple absolute – the most common type of freehold estate ownership. This gives the owner and any heirs rights such as:

  -The authority to live in, rent or mortgage the property

  -The authority to sell, destroy, or reassign ownership of the property

  -The authority to construct buildings on the property

  -The authority to excavate minerals, gas, and oil

  -The authority to refuse the use of property by others

- **Fee tail** – restricts the sale or inheritance of an estate.
- **Non freehold estate** – an estate similar to a lease or contract that holds limited rights and usage to the property and typically has a set or predetermined time for the tenant. It is not inheritable.
- **Fee upon condition** – the fees/taxes of the property are based on outside circumstances such as home modifications, outside liens or holds on the property, or changes in the real estate market.
- **Life estate** – an estate that ends at the death of the owner and reverts to the original owner. The owner of the life estate is called the life tenant, and is designated ownership of the land for the duration of his life.
- *Pur autre vie* – "for another's life" - similar to a life estate, it states that a person's interest will last for another person's lifetime instead of his own.
- **Remainderman** – an individual who inherits property when an estate is terminated by the former owner. This typically happens due to the death of the estate's owner, but can also be a voluntary act.
- **Life estate in reversion** – a life estate ownership that 'reverts' to the original owner or grantor.
- **Estate for years** – estate with a specific duration, such as an agreement between landlord and tenant.
- **Estate from year to year** – estate that has a duration that is indefinite, as with leases that carry over.
- **Concurrent estates** – estates that two or more people own or possess at the same time. This includes joint tenancy, tenancy in common, and tenancy by entirety.

When an estate is transferred between parties, it is usually done in one of two ways:

Deeds – Deeds can be transferred from one party to another, usually through the county office and completed while both parties are present; this process is usually voluntary but can be involuntary if ordered by a court of law. Lost deeds require the county's superior court to establish that a deed copy is true. The deed holder must file an affidavit saying that a thorough search was made.

Will/inheritance – Deeds transferred after the original owner dies and designates the property to another party; if a party is not assigned, the government can take control of the land and use it as it sees fit (putting it up for sale, or reassigning survey lines).

Public Controls

- **Police power** – The government may restrict use of property with police power. The laws are created to protect the public, and they include rent control, zoning, and safety codes. Losses due to the exercise of police power are not compensated.
- **Eminent domain** – The government has the authority to take ownership through the exercise of eminent domain. The land is converted to public use such as parks, utilities, and schools. The owner is compensated for eminent domain.
  - Condemnation – Used when negotiation fails, condemnation is the process of legally taking eminent domain and paying full value for the property.
  - Severance damage – The amount paid to a property owner if a piece of land is taken under condemnation.
  - Inverse condemnation – Property owners can file suit to make the government buy damaged property. This may occur even when the government does not exercise the right to eminent domain.
  - Consequential damage – The money awarded when the government causes property damage. The damages are paid but the land is not purchased.
- **Environmental hazards and regulations** – Laws to protect people and the environment are enacted on the federal and state level. Federal laws include:
  - The Clean Air Act – The act was passed in 1970 and amended in 1990. The act gives the Environmental Protection Agency (EPA) authority to monitor emissions.
  - The Clean Water Act – This act, passed in 1972, authorizes the EPA to monitor water quality and issue National Poison Data System permits to organizations that cause pollution.
  - National Environmental Policy Act (NEPA) – passed in 1969 after the Santa Barbara oil spill, this act makes the entity of the property responsible for ensuring the safety of the environment, including pollution and accidents.
  - Comprehensive Environmental Response, Compensation, and Liability Act (CERCLA) – passed in 1980, it was designed to be a 'superfund' that supplies resources to hazardous waste sites, such as oil or contaminant spills. Through CERCLA, entities responsible for the spill are also responsible for the cleanup.
  - The Endangered Species Act – passed in 1973 and designed to provide protection for wildlife and flora that are at risk of becoming extinct; it states that animals considered endangered are not allowed to be hunted or harmed and that state government can seize any land that is needed to preserve the species.

- The Safe Drinking Water Act – Passed in 1974, the act sets standards for drinking water safety. Amended in 1986 and 1996, water sources such as lakes and rivers are also protected.
- The Toxic Substances Control Act – Enacted in 1976, the act allows the EPA to regulate the safety of new and existing chemicals in the marketplace.
- Residential Lead-Based Paint Hazard Reduction Act – Passed in 1992, the act is used to protect people from lead in paint, soil, and dust.
- Flood plain regulations: Floodways adjoin flood plains, which will discharge the regulatory flood. Flood plains are typically mapped by state and local governments. This allows for flood proofing with the construction of barriers in development review.
- Fire codes: Fire hazards are regulated by the International Fire Code, and require egress. The US has adopted the National Fire Prevention Code, the Standard Fire Prevention Code, and the Uniform Fire Code.

Private Controls:

- **Restrictive covenants** – Also called deed restrictions, privately limit the use of property and are often established by developers. Restrictions can include everything from structures to landscaping.
- **Homeowners association (HOA)** – Homeowners associations are corporations or private parties established by a real estate developer. They demand that homeowners become members, and ownership may be lost if dues are not paid.
  - Conditions – Restrictions that determine actions owners must take are conditions.
  - Covenants – Owners make promises or covenants regarding properties.
  - Restrictions – Limitations placed on the homeowner by the developer or homeowners' association.

Water Rights

State law and the source of the water determine the water rights. When the water can be navigated, the ownership extends to the mean waterline at the boundary. It extends to the center of the water if it is not possible to navigate. Underground streams are governed by the same rules as surface streams if they can be discovered easily.

Although water rights vary by state, there are two that are common nationwide:

- **Riparian rights** – When dealing with a navigable body of water, the property owner's boundary will reach to the water's accretion line. With a non-navigable body of water, the property owner's boundary will stop at the water's center point.
- **Littoral rights** – Take into consideration the rights of a property owner whose land shares a border with a non-flowing body of water like a lake or ocean.
- Other terms of water rights:

- Accretion – Natural deposit of soil that results in the steady increase in land
- Avulsion – When water abruptly changes its course, the rapid decrease in land that results
- Erosion – When water, wind and other natural elements cause a steady decrease in land
- Reliction – When the retreat of water causes a steady increase in land
- Alluvion – When water shifts soil to another person's land
- Accession – Attaining land due to the soil deposited by natural elements

Other Nationally Recognized Water Rights:

- **Natural flow doctrine** –If a riparian owner's use of the water causes the water to diminish in amount, quality, or pace, that use can be stopped. All riparian owners have the right to have access to the water in its natural state.
- **Doctrine of reasonable use** – Each riparian owner is entitled to reasonable use of the water. Unless one owner's use severely inhibits another owner's use, it cannot be stopped. Reasonable use can be determined by assessing changes to water quantity, quality, velocity, and pollution, among other things.
- **Doctrine of prior appropriation** - Refers to water rights that are not linked to land ownership. They can be sold and mortgaged in the same way as other property.
- **Doctrine of beneficial use** – States that the first users of the water have priority, but they must use the water in a beneficial manner, within a reasonable time frame.
- **Doctrine of correlative rights** – Imposes a limit on landowners regarding their share of the water. Generally, this limit is based on the share of land owned by each.

Property Conditions

Property Condition Disclosure Forms

Usually before signing a purchase agreement, but at least before closing, salespersons/brokers are required to provide potential buyers with a document that explains the condition of the property they want to buy, and it must include all material facts. If the proper disclosures (varies per state) have not been made, the purchase contract may become unenforceable. It is also important that salespersons/brokers rather than giving their own description of the property condition, should encourage the potential buyers to have a professional inspection done, and this should be included in the disclosure form.

Other Disclosures

Real estate agents must disclose their position to the buyers and sellers. Latent defects that may not be seen in an inspection are considered material defects in some states. The environment and crime risks may also be required disclosures. Seller warranties may be requested by the buyer and guarantee that the seller has not withheld any information about the property. The Real Estate Seller Disclosure Law requires the seller to inform the buyer of any material defect. This is balanced by the Home Inspection Law, which makes it the buyer's duty to hire a home inspector. The law recognizes inspectors who follow the standards of practices and code of ethics established by national home inspector associations.

The need for inspection

There are many instances in which having an inspection would be warranted, although it is not carried out. For the real estate purchaser, it is advisable that a thorough, professional inspection is done before agreeing to purchase the property. Not doing so could result in costly repairs down the line for the buyer, or even legal action against the real estate company.

Property Value

Why an Appraisal?

The first step to performing an appraisal is finding out why it should be done. Here are the more common reasons:

- **Condemnation**: In cases where the government uses eminent domain to acquire property, the owner must be compensated at fair market value.
- **Assessed value**: In order to determine the property taxes that must be paid on the property.
- **Insurance:** So the insurance company can establish what it will pay for a loss.
- **Estate settlement:** In order to verify the value of a deceased individual's estate.
- **Sales value for owner:** To determine how much the property should be sold for.
- **Loan value:** To establish the maximum loan amount that can be secured by the property.
- **Exchanges:** In cases where the owner of a property is going to trade for another property instead of selling.

Value and Analysis:

Value

The value of land is constantly changing. It is affected by the actions of both the buyers and the sellers.. The market value is that which a buyer and seller are likely to agree on for the exchange. The market value requires an understanding of the property's condition by each party, access to normal financing in the area, and a requirement that neither party act under duress.

- **Cost** – The cost is the money an owner pays into purchasing and altering the property.
- **Sales price** – The price that someone pays to purchase property may be less than the cost.

There are different ways to assess and assign value to property:

- **Assessed value** – The value given by the county assessor for the purpose of imposing property tax is assessed value.
- **Book value** – The depreciation of property cost for tax purposes determines the book value.
- **Insurance value** – The insurance assigns a maximum value that the company is willing to pay.
- **Investment value** – The amount of money that investors are willing to provide for investment properties.
- **Loan value** – The amount of a loan that can be secured by a property.
- **Salvage value** – This value is determined by choosing the value of structures and improvements after they are removed. This value is the cost less accumulated depreciation.

What Affects Value:

- **Environmental factors** – Any environmental changes will alter value. For example, pollution or natural disasters will cause the value to plummet.
- **Externality** – Outside factors such as interest rates, commercial construction, and education levels of residents affect value. Externalities may be positive or negative.
- **Supply and demand** – High demand and low supply increase the property value.
- **Life cycle** – Every property and neighborhood have a natural life cycle. The life cycle has four possible stages:
  - Development – The first stage is typically a time of growth.
  - Equilibrium – The value of the property reaches its height.
  - Decline – The property loses value.
  - Revitalization – The values improve with renovations.

Principles of Value

The principles of value are used in the process of appraising property values.

- **Anticipation** – The anticipation that the current value of a property is going to increase due to future benefits is used in appraisal.
- **Assemblage (also called plottage)** – Combining plots of land together to create larger properties may increase value.
- **Change** – Value is always affected by change. Physical changes are caused over time by environmental factors. Political change will affect regulations and restrictions. Economic changes are related to prosperity levels, and social changes occur with shifting demographics.
- **Conformity** – Similarities and conformity to neighboring properties increase the value in appraisals. This applies in residential and commercial properties.
- **Competition** – This principle is related to an increase in demand and profits, which increases competition.
- **Highest and best use** – The most profitable use that a property is legally allowed.
- **Law of decreasing returns** – The point at which improvements no longer sufficiently increase the value of the property.

- **Law of increasing returns** – This occurs when improvements make sufficient contributions to the value of the property.
- **Progression** – The value of a property increases when it is located near highly valued properties.
- **Regression** – The value of a property decreases when it is located in a neighborhood of lower-valued properties.
- **Substitution** – The maximum value of a property is determined by the value of an equal property. When an income-producing property is valued, the term applied is opportunity cost, which means that the property value is equal to other, similar investments.
- **Theory of distribution** – This is the understanding that the property value is greater when the land, labor, capital, and management of a property are balanced.

Methods of Estimating Value or Appraisal

There are three basic methods that appraisers use to determine the value of a property. The property itself will determine which approach should be used. The three methods are market data, cost, and income approach.

Market Data

The market data approach is also called the direct sales comparison. It determines value by comparing the property to similar properties that have sold recently. The appraiser must choose three comparable properties, or "comps," that sold in the past six months to estimate value of the appraised or subject property. The comps should have as many corresponding features as possible such as the same number of bedrooms. Adjustments may be made if there are no matching comps in the area.

Cost Approach

The cost approach is used when there are no market comps and the property will not generate income. It estimates value by deducting the accrued depreciation from the estimated cost of improvements, known as the replacement cost. Reproduction cost, which is the cost to duplicate an asset or structure, may be used in place of the replacement cost.

The depreciation that appraisers must consider includes physical deterioration, functional obsolescence, and environmental/economic depreciation. Physical deterioration is normal wear and tear, but it also includes the effect of the elements and breakdown. Functional obsolescence occurs when there is a defect in design or the design and amenities are outdated. Both functional obsolescence and physical deterioration may be curable or incurable.

- Curable – This type of depreciation may be altered with repairs.
- Incurable – This type of depreciation may not be altered by repairs.

The land value is also a crucial part in determining the overall property value.

Environmental/economic depreciation is caused by outside factors such as the environment or social factors. This type of depreciation is not curable.

Formula

Value = Replacement or Reproduction Cost – Accrued Depreciation + Land Value

Income Approach

This approach is commonly used with income properties. The income generated by the property is used to estimate the value by capitalization. This requires the net operating income and capitalization rate. The operating income is money left after the expenses are paid. The location of the property and the market will determine the capitalization rate.

Formula

Value = Net operating income ÷ Capitalization rate

The Purpose of Appraisal and How It Is Used

The appraisal is necessary to determine value. The value, however, is estimated by a professional who documents the findings. The appraisal should reflect the market value or fair market value. There are five necessary factors that determine if there is fair market value for a property:

- The property should be purchased with cash or the equivalent
- The property is not on the market for an unusual time period.
- Both the seller and buyer understand the conditions and uses of the property.
- The seller has the right to transfer the title.
- Neither the buyer nor seller enter the sale under duress.

Appraiser's Role

The appraiser must complete seven steps in the process of appraisal.

- State the problem – Establish the nature and purpose of the appraisal.
- Determine the kinds and sources of data necessary – Consider the property characteristics, economic and other factors, appropriate approaches, and data needed.
- Determine the highest and best use of the site.
- Estimate the value of the site.
- Estimate the property's value by each of the appropriate approaches (market data, cost, and/or income.)

- Reconcile the different values – Termed reconciliation or correlation, estimates market value using the different approaches.
- Report the value to the client in writing – Use the narrative appraisal approach (discusses the factors used and reasons for a conclusion); a form report (computer generated forms, typically used for single residences such as the Uniform Residential Report); reports written in the Uniform Standards of Professional Appraisal Practice; the self-contained report (a complete narrative appraisal); a summary report (a narrative appraisal with less detail); and a restricted report (a report with minimal information).

Competitive or Comparative Market Analysis (CMA)

In some states, real estate brokers have the authority to prepare property appraisals. In doing so, the broker must be sure to follow the uniform standards as well as inform the potential buyer that the CMA is not an appraisal. The purpose of the CMA is to allow the homeowner (seller) and potential buyer to have property range of value in a particular area for a certain period of time. With CMA, properties that have sold and those that are listed but have not sold are used.

Given the range of asking/purchase prices of all the properties, the homeowner (seller) has a more accurate picture of the asking price. A seller who asks for more than what is realistic may not attract much interest, which could in turn prevent him from having a buyer. The potential buyer also has an idea of what a fair offer would be. A potential buyer who offers an amount that is lower than what is fair may insult the seller and lose the opportunity to purchase the property or even negotiate.

Important Contracts/Documents

A contract is executory when the duties under it have not been completely fulfilled. A contract is executed when the duties under it have been completely fulfilled.

The types of contracts/documents are:

Listing: Details of agreement between a brokerage and homeowner regarding the sale of a particular property.

Offer to Purchase: Typically, a fill-in-the-blank format, displays the terms of the sale of a property, such as price. Contingencies are also included.

Purchase & Sale Agreement: Thoroughly explains the responsibilities of each party in the Offer to Purchase. This document is usually signed once the buyer has completed a home inspection.

Occupancy Agreement: A contract that gives the buyer permission to move into a property before escrow.

Lease: Contract between a renter and owner/manager. The renter is entitled to use the property for the time outlined in the contract (lease).

Invitation to treat: Invitation to open negotiations.

Deed: Written document that transfers title to real property.

Mortgage note: An IOU that spells out the terms by which the borrower agrees to repay the loan.

Mortgage deed: Explains the collateral (the property) to be used to secure repayment of debt in case of default.

Bilateral contract: Both parties have responsibilities to fulfill.

Unilateral contract: Only one party has responsibilities to fulfill.

In order to be valid, contracts should:

- Include an offer and acceptance
- Explain the consideration to be used (does not have to be money)
- Outline the objective; must be legal
- Involve competent parties
- Include addresses
- Be written (unless lease is for a year or less), according to the Statute of Frauds
- Be signed by both parties, giving their consent
- Have date and place
- Have a description of property
-

Financing

What is the Cycle of Real Estate?

1. The property is listed

2. The buyer is qualified

3. The buyer is shown the property

4. The agreement between the buyer and seller is signed

5. The buyer finalizes and secures financing

6. The closing occurs

Mortgage Markets

The two types of mortgage markets are primary and secondary. In the primary market, loans are made directly to borrowers. In the secondary market, the loans that are executed in the primary market are sold to investors.

Common Home Loan Purchasers in Secondary Market:

- The Federal National Mortgage Association (Fannie Mae) – purchases all types of home loans.
- The Federal Home Loan Mortgage Corporation (Freddie Mac) – purchases conventional loans.
- The Government National Mortgage Association (Ginnie Mae) – purchases FHA and VA loans.

Conventional loans: Private loans that have no insurance backing from the government. The lender expects the borrower to pay back the loan or undergo a foreclosure of the property.

Government Programs

VA-guaranteed loans: Loans that are backed by the US Department of Veterans Affairs that the lender will be compensated for in the case of the borrower defaulting. In order to be eligible for such a loan, the individual must be a veteran who has been issued a certificate of eligibility by the VA. In addition, the home the borrower wants to buy must be appraised by a professional approved by the VA, and be issued a certificate of reasonable value. Other stipulations regarding the holders of VA-guaranteed loans are:

- The loan can only be for one-to-four family, owner-occupied residences.
- There may be a funding fee associated with the loan, depending on the veteran's category and down payment. The funding fee is typically 0 – 10%, but can be more.
- Prepayment penalties cannot be assessed.
- Although the property can be sold later to another veteran or non-veteran, the current borrower must get a "release of liability" notice from the VA so that he is not held liable for future foreclosure or deficiency.

Federal Housing Administration (FHA) loans: Loans are administered through the US Housing and Urban Development (HUD) and protect the lender in case the borrower defaults on the loan.

Stipulations regarding FHA loans are:

- The FHA decides on the maximum loan amounts.
- During closing, the borrower must pay an upfront mortgage insurance premium.
- Prepayment penalties cannot be assessed.
- The loan can only be for one-to-four family, owner-occupied residences.
- These loans may be assumed. However, if a new borrower assumes the loan of an existing borrower, both would be responsible in the case of a deficiency due to a foreclosure.
- Lower than normal down payments may be acceptable. However, if the borrower puts down less than 20%, he may be required to purchase private mortgage insurance.

Construction loan – Given to a developer or builder on a short-term basis. Funds are received according to construction completion phases. Once finished, the builder/developer must obtain long term financing.

Blanket mortgage – A developer or contractor borrows funds to purchase several lots of land. A release clause is common, which means the developer/contractor can sell a land parcel while maintaining the mortgage on the rest of the property.

Package mortgage – Personal property and real estate are used as collateral.

Demand mortgage – Allows the lender to require payment whenever it wants to.

Purchase money mortgage – The seller of the property is financing for the buyer.

Junior (second) mortgage – Loan in addition to the primary mortgage. In cases of default, this loan may or may not be paid, depending on whether the primary loan is fully paid.

Open-end mortgage – Gives the borrower the option of borrowing additional funds on top of what is initially borrowed, up to a certain amount, without having to complete documentation to rewrite the mortgage.

Wraparound mortgage – Merge a new loan and existing loan. Payment is made on both mortgages to the wraparound mortgagee, who then forwards the payments to the appropriate mortgagee.

Variable (adjustable) rate mortgage – Over the life of the loan, the interest rate can increase or decrease, depending on the Treasury Bill Index. There is a cap set on how much the rate can increase during each rate change period and over the life of loan.

Balloon loan – Starts off charging a lower than normal fixed-rate interest, but after a certain amount of time, will "balloon." The time at which the loan balloons varies with each lender, but is typically 5, 7, or 10 years. Once the loan balloons, the borrower must pay off the loan.

Shared equity loan – The lender provides the funds at a low interest rate in exchange for a portion of the property's equity.

Equity loan – A second mortgage. It is used to access the equity in the home.

Negative amortization – The interest rate on an adjustable rate mortgage increases, but the payment each month stays the same. This results in inadequate payment for the monthly principal and interest, and the deficit amount is added to the outstanding principal balance.

Term loan – Loan that is interest only. The total loan amount is due at the maturity date.

Fully amortized loan – Loan that is principal and interest. At the maturity date, the loan will have been paid in full.

Partially amortized loan – Loan that is principal and interest. This is short term, so a balloon payment will be made at the maturity date.

Fixed rate loan – The same interest rate is charged over the life of loan. Term, fully amortized, and partially amortized loans can include this feature.

How Does the Buyer Secure Financing?

Once the buyer completes a mortgage application, the lender (savings and loan association, commercial bank, mutual savings bank, cooperative bank, credit union, mortgage company, life insurance company, or private lender) completes several steps in deciding whether or not to approve the application. These steps are: 1. Have an appraisal done of the property 2. Evaluate the buyer's potential to pay the loan 3. Review the buyer's credit history.

Purchase and Sale Agreement forms typically include a financing clause which is language included in the form to protect the buyer in case he does not receive the funding necessary to purchase the property. If funding is not received, he can withdraw his application and receive any earnest money deposits.

Terms regarding funding

Discount rate – Interest rate charged by the Federal Reserve Bank to financial institutions.

Prime rate – Interest rate charged by banks to preferred borrowers.

Mortgage rates – Rates used for long-term secured loans.

Origination points – Fee paid by borrowers for a loan being approved. Each point is 1% of the loan.

Discount points – Paid by the borrower at the start of the loan in order to get a lower interest rate for the life of the loan.

Truth in Lending Act – Enacted by Congress in 1968 as a part of the Consumer Protection Act. Also known as Regulation Z, it applies to lenders who conduct more than 25 consumer credit transactions in a year, have more than five transactions in a year with a residence used as a security, and/or offer credit to consumers.

Equal Credit Opportunity Act – Creditors are prohibited from discriminating against applicants on the basis of race, color, religion, national origin, sex, marital status, or age.

Home Mortgage Disclosure Act – Financial institutions are required to make annual disclosures about home purchases, refinances, etc. regarding one-to-four-unit residences.

Community Reinvestment Act – Promotes the idea that commercial banks and savings associations work to help fulfill the financial needs of consumers in all areas, low to high income.

Fair Credit Reporting Act – The collection, disbursement, and utilization of consumer information is regulated via this act.

Fair and Accurate Credit Transactions Act – Once every 12 months, consumers are able to obtain a free credit report from each of the credit reporting agencies (Equifax, Experian, and TransUnion).

Gramm-Leach-Bliley Act – Financial institutions are required to safeguard the sensitive information of their consumers as well as explain the company's information-sharing practices.

Contracts/Agency

Leases

Leases are enforceable when signed by both the landlord and tenant. Leases include a description of the property and do not have to be recorded. The Uniform Residential Landlord and Tenant Act is used in many states to simplify leases and make them more uniform.

Common lease types:

- **Gross lease** – States that the landlord is responsible for paying expenses (i.e. property taxes, insurance, and maintenance costs). Apartment complexes typically use this type of lease.

- **Net lease** – States that the tenant is responsible for paying expenses (i.e. property taxes, insurance, and maintenance costs).

- **Percentage lease** – States that the tenant will pay a percentage of gross sales as rent as well as a base rental amount. This lease is usually used in properties such as shopping centers.

- **Office building lease** – A combination of a gross and net lease. The initial expenses are paid by the landlord, then each tenant pays a *pro rata* share of the expenses that exceed that.

- **Graduated lease** – Records changes that take place in rent (increase or decrease) over the lease's term.

- **Ninety-nine-year lease** – Used in such cases as when the owner does not want to sell, or the tenant wants to use funds on capital improvements. Often used for commercial development.

- **Leveraged lease** – A lease is financed by a third party loan. The lessee pays the lessor who pays the third party.

Leases may be assigned, meaning the individual who originally signed the lease as lessee transfers the remaining lease to a third party. Another option is to sublet, which often means only part of the lease is transferred. Whether the original lessee assigns or sublets a lease, he or she is still obligated to honor the lease. In order to remove the original lessee as the responsible party, novation, in which the original lease is replaced by a new lease, must be done. Not all leases allow transfer to another lessee.

Tenancy

Tenancy at will – An indefinite rental period that is agreed on or occurs when there is no tenancy for duration.

Tenancy at sufferance – A tenant keeps possession of the property without the consent of the landlord.

Tenancy for years – A written lease specifies the duration of tenancy.

Periodic tenancy – The lease is set for certain periods, such as year-to-year or month-to-month.

What are the Obligations of the Lessor and Lessee?

Lessor:

- Utility services (lessee typically has to pay for these services, but the lessor must make them available)
- Property that is inhabitable
- Property that does not violate sanitary and/or building codes
- Quiet enjoyment of the property
- No interference with the lessee's right to a constructive eviction if property is uninhabitable or lessor does not allow quiet enjoyment of the property
- After collection of a security deposit from the lessee (must be deposited into an interest-bearing account) and the lessee lives in the apartment for two years or more, the lessee is entitled to the interest paid by the bank.

Lessee:

Use the property in the proper manner:

- Keep the property clean
- Use property appliances and fixtures as they are designed to be used
- Do not destroy property or allow others to do so
- Pay for damage to property.

A property is not considered habitable in the following situations:

- Known carbon monoxide leak
- Hot water heater is not safe
- Lead paint that is not disclosed

- Plumbing difficulties
- Mold conditions

Tenants have a responsibility to inform landlords if repairs are needed and must give reasonable access for repairs. Reasonable time for property repairs is typically 30 days.

Commercial property may require tenants to make repairs. In this situation, the landlord may provide a Schedule of Dilapidations listing necessary repairs and maintenance.

Tenant may withhold rent when the defects are: not the fault of the tenant, serious, communicated to the landlord, affect health and safety, and the landlord has had a reasonable period of time to fix the problem. The defect cannot cost more than a month's rent, and withholding can only be used twice in a year.

Property may also be abandoned when the defects are: not the fault of the tenant, serious, communicated to the landlord, affect health and safety, and the landlord has had a reasonable period of time to fix the problem. This is more likely to happen with expensive problems that require more than a month's rent.

Constructive eviction: When the property is uninhabitable, the tenant must provide written notice and allow the landlord to fix the problems in a reasonable time. Unresolved problems provide the tenant an opportunity to leave and no longer owe rent.

Eviction

Virginia requires that tenants with leases of one year or less be given a five-day notice before filing for eviction for any reason other than nonpayment of rent. A lease for longer than a year requires a notice of 30 days.

Security deposits may not be more than two months' rent in the state of Virginia. Landlords may not charge pet deposits if the tenant requires a service animal, because it would violate the Fair Housing Laws.

Management

Property managers are assigned through service contracts to serve as the landlord's agent. The contract requires the date and signature of the owner and manager. Corporation ownership requires the corporate name and seal on the contract. Managers owe the owners fiduciary duties. They may be paid in flat fees or percentage fees.

There are three types of managers:

- Broker who manages multiple properties
- Building manager
- Resident manager

Property managers may need management or real estate licenses, depending on the state they live in and the required responsibilities. Overseeing leases typically requires real estate licensing. Managers are in charge of maintenance, which includes creating a maintenance plan, keeping records, and overseeing activities. It is also the manager's responsibility to oversee the budget and keep costs down. When outsourcing maintenance, the manager can ask for a(n):

- RFP: Request for proposal (includes comprehensive information)
- RFQ: Request for quotation (used for simple, inexpensive situations)
- RFI: Request for information
- RFSQ: Request for supplier qualifications

Property managers are also responsible for reconciling bank statements, managing records, and sending monthly owner's updates that include reports on income, expenses, building, and tenants.

Options

An option allows an individual to purchase a property at a certain amount if done within a specified time frame. Options are created by the property owner getting a written agreement and being paid. Options are assignable without approval from the property owner.

Purchase and Sale Agreement

There are several key elements included on the Purchase and Sale Agreement to make it valid. These are:

- The names of all parties involved

- A land description

- The sales price

- The amount of earnest money provided by the buyer

- The contract date

- Buyer and seller signatures

The Virginia Statute of Frauds says that the Purchase and Sale Agreements must be in writing. The exception to this rule is for a lease that will be enforced for a year or less from the contract date. Once signed, the buyer has equitable title, which means he has interest in the property even though the transaction is not fully complete. Once the transaction is fully complete, the buyer has legal title to the property which gives him all of the rights associated with it.

The majority of Purchase and Sale Agreements give buyers the "right to assign," which means they can assign the contract to someone else. However, they are not off the hook for the requirements of the contract in the case where the new assignee does not fulfill his duties under the contract.

Breach of Contract

A breach of contract is when one party to a contract fails to uphold his duties outlined in the contract. When this occurs, the party who is aggrieved can be compensated by doing the following:

- Suing for monetary damages

- Suing for the party who breached the contract to fulfill his duties under the contract

- If the seller is the one wronged, he can sue for liquidated money damages (i.e. keeping the earnest money deposit)

- Both parties agreeing to annul the contract

Termination of an Offer

A purchase offer can be terminated if one of the following conditions exists:

- Either of the parties dies

- The timeframe of the offer expires

- The offeror revokes before being informed that the offeree accepts

- Either party becomes bankrupt

- The property is destroyed or condemned

- The offeree rejects a counteroffer

Counteroffers are used in response to the initial offer regarding the sale/purchase of a property. The individual to whom the counteroffer is made may immediately agree with the counteroffer or further negotiate until a mutually agreed upon offer is reached.

Agency Law

An agent is the one who represents the fiduciary interest of his/her client. There are two types of agencies: single and dual. In a single agency, the agent works on behalf of either the buyer or seller. In a dual agency, the agent works on behalf of the buyer and seller. In the case of a dual agency in the Commonwealth of Virginia; the agent must have written consent from the buyer and seller that they are aware of and agree to the arrangement. The agent (in a dual agency situation) cannot offer all fiduciary duties to both clients.

The fiduciary duties are (remember OLD CAR):

Obedience

Loyalty

Disclosure (of material facts concerning the transaction)

Confidentiality

Accountability (of funds)

Reasonable care

A real estate company can be set up so that either all agents in the company have the same relationship with the customer OR only the agent listed on the disclosure form can represent the customer.

In Virginia, there are several relationship options between the agent and potential buyer or seller. These are:

- Seller's agent – Represents the seller in all aspects of the transaction and owes all fiduciary duties to the seller.

- Buyer's agent – Represents the buyer in all aspects of the transaction and owes all fiduciary duties to the buyer.

- Facilitator – Brings the buyer and seller together but does not act on behalf of either party as agent. Does not owe fiduciary duties to either party.

- Designated seller's and buyer's agent – Represents his/her client (either the buyer or seller) and owes all fiduciary duties to client. If the client agrees, the agent can be "designated" as the client's only agent. In Virginia, this must be in writing.

- Dual agent – Represents the buyer and seller. All fiduciary duties cannot be given to either party. In Virginia, this must be in writing and signed by both the buyer and seller. Also in Virginia, it is unlawful to have an undisclosed dual agency.

Listing Types

Open: States that the broker will get paid a commission if she secures a buyer, which results in the sale of the property. This can be done between a seller and as many brokers as she would like. If the listing broker does not sell the home, but rather the homeowner or another broker sell it, the listing broker does not get paid the commission.

Exclusive agency: The seller can enter into agreement to sell with only one broker. If the broker actively sells the house or the house is sold through the Multiple Listing Service (MLS), the broker will be paid the commission. If the homeowner sells the house on his own, he will not pay commission to the broker.

Exclusive right to sell: States the listing broker will receive the commission on the sale of the property regardless of who actually sells it.

Net: States that the homeowner will receive a specific amount from the sale of the property. Anything received over that amount will go to the listing broker. This type of arrangement is illegal in Virginia.

Multiple Listing Service (MLS): System used to display information all members have with regard to real estate they have for sale.

Termination of Agency

Agency contracts can be terminated by:

- completion of the objective

- time limit expiration

- rescission

- revocation

- death of the principal or broker

- property destruction

- bankruptcy of either party

How are agents paid?

Agents receive payment for services by working under some type of agreement (i.e. contract, listing agreement, or buyer-agency representation agreement).

What is a commission split?

When properties are sold, the commission paid for the sale may be divided among many parties. This can include a co-broker, broker-owner, and agent. Different real estate offices choose various ways to split the commission. For example, some offices take off the top a fee that covers operating expenses, while others may charge the agent a set monthly fee that takes care of overhead.

Licensing requirements in Virginia

Read – Virginia Department of Professional and Occupational Regulation:
http://www.dpor.virginia.gov/Boards/Real-Estate/Pre-License/

What does the Real Estate Board do?

The Board, which is appointed by the governor, consists of nine members. Seven are people who have significant experience as real estate licensees, and must have had a salesperson's license for five consecutive years before their appointment. Two are people with a "recognized interest in consumer affairs," and cannot be real estate professionals. The Board elects a chairperson from its membership.

Every member of the Board serves for four years. The Board must meet at least monthly and must have four members present to have a quorum and conduct business.

The Virginia Board has the authority to do many things:

- Carry out state law.

- Administer examinations.

- Review records.

- Enforce license law by having hearings and if necessary, appeals.

- Give, refuse, and revoke licenses.

When would an agent's license be temporarily or permanently taken away or refused for renewal? If he:

- Willingly makes misrepresentations

- Serves as broker and undisclosed principal in one transaction

- Serves as a dual agent without receiving written permission from the buyer and seller

- Does not account for received funds within an acceptable timeframe

- Compensates an unlicensed individual with a commission

- Does not report a criminal conviction

- Provided false information on the initial license application or renewal form

- Engages in real estate activities with an expired license

- Engages in real estate activities while in an impaired state

- Participates in a net listing

- Participates in discriminatory practices

- Does not supply a real estate contract copy to all of the appropriate parties

- Commingles business and personal funds

- Encourages a party to a contract to break it in order to benefit himself

- Receives, gives, or charges a hidden fee on expenses for a principal

If there is a hearing with regard to an agent's license, records and witnesses may be permissible. The licensee must be informed about the hearing (in a written format) a minimum of 10 days before the hearing is scheduled to be held. If the licensee appears for the hearing, she can be represented by counsel. She can also ask questions of witnesses present. If the licensee is not satisfied with the decision of the Board, an appeal to the superior court within 20 days is acceptable. If in the end, the licensee still loses her license, she has seven days to release it to the Board.

There are many activities in Virginia related to real estate that require a license to perform when a fee is charged. These include:

- sales
- exchanges
- purchases
- rentals/leases
- negotiations
- offers
- listings
- options
- advertising real property
- prospecting
- loan negotiating
- apartment searching

What activities do not require a real estate license?

- Person acting on his own behalf
- Property manager employed by property owner
- Auctioneer who is licensed as such
- Trustee
- Public servant executing official duties
- Attorney-in-fact under power of attorney
- Court appointee
- Financial institution employees (bank, insurance company, or credit union)

What Are the Types of Licenses?

Real Estate Broker: For a fee, this individual performs the above activities for another person.

Real Estate Salesperson: Individual cannot perform negotiations but can perform the other above activities. A salesperson must always work for an employer broker. If the salesperson is a nonresident, she can hold a Virginia real estate license, but is required to file a power of attorney designating the Chairman of the Board as attorney-in-fact. This is necessary in case the salesperson is facing any legal actions.

What Makes One Eligible for Licensing?

An individual is eligible for a salesperson license if he:

- Is at least 18-years-old

- Fulfills 60 hours of approved coursework

- Pays the $170 application fee

- Pays the $60 exam fee

- Successfully completes the state and national portions of the salesperson's exam

- Applies for a license within one year of passing the exam

An individual salesperson is eligible for an Associate Broker or Broker's license if he:

- Is at least 18-years-old

- Provides proof of having been an active salesperson for 36 of the past 48 months

- Fulfills 180 hours of approved coursework, including at least three broker-specific courses

- Successfully completes the state and national portions of the broker exam

- Pays the application fee of $210

If a licensed broker (also the sole proprietor) of a real estate agency dies, the broker's representative must apply with the Board and will be issued a temporary license. The completion of an exam is not necessary. The license is non-renewable and good up to one year from the date of the original broker's death.

Under normal circumstances, a real estate license is valid for two years. It must be renewed before the last day of the month in which the license was issued. Within one year of earning the license, new salespersons must complete 30 continuing education hours. These continuing education hours consist of eight courses. As of January 1, 2014, there is only one approved education provider for these hours in Virginia. Salespersons that do not complete the continuing education courses will have their licenses put in an "inactive status." With an "inactive" license, individuals can earn and collect referral fees, but cannot practice real estate. In addition to completing continuing education course hours, to renew a license, individuals must pay the renewal fee within 30 days of the license's expiration. If a license remains expired for one year, it may not be reinstated for any reason.

Virginia has real estate license reciprocity with the 49 other states. To apply for a salesperson's license through reciprocity, the applicant must hold a current active salesperson's license in another state. The applicant must then pass the state portion of the real estate licensing exam, complete the 60-hour course called "Principles of Real Estate," and provide three letters of certification from the other jurisdiction where he is licensed. Brokers may also apply for licensing via reciprocity in Virginia. In order to apply for a broker's license via reciprocity in Virginia, applicants must hold a current broker's license in another state. Applicants for a broker's license must pass the state portion of the licensing exam, provide verification of experience as an active salesperson for 36 out of the last 48 months, submit transcripts for the institution(s) at which the 180 hours of education were completed, and provide three letters of certification from the other jurisdiction where he is licensed.

After the initial granting of the license, both salespersons and brokers have continuing education requirements for future renewals. Salespersons must take 16 hours of continuing education in every renewal period. Eight of these hours are on required topics and the remaining eight are the licensee's choice from a list of approved courses. Of those eight hours, three must be in ethics and standards of conduct, two must be in fair housing, and one hour each must be taken in Legal Updates and Emerging Trends, Real Estate Agency, and Real Estate Contracts. Brokers must take 24 hours of continuing education. These courses will be the same as the salesperson's required courses, plus an eight-hour broker-specific course.

Statutory Requirements Governing Activities of Licensees

Advertising requirements:

- Misleading or false advertising by brokers is prohibited

- Advertising without disclosing the fact that the broker is a real estate broker is forbidden

- Advertising property under the salesperson's name is not allowed

- Advertising that's done in a way that directly or indirectly discriminates against any group is prohibited

Salespersons cannot be self-employed, but must be hired by a real estate broker as an employee or independent contractor. Brokers can compensate salespersons through payment, fees, or commissions. Brokers are responsible for the actions of their salespersons.

Brokers are also responsible for maintaining a place of business and making the Board aware of any changes regarding location. A copy of the broker's license must be displayed in an area of the office that is visible to the public. In addition, the broker must let the Board know all of the agents affiliated with the firm. If an agent leaves, the Board must be informed and if a new agent joins the firm, the Board must be informed.

Virginia and Promotional Sales of Out-of-State Real Property

- Real property located in a state other than Virginia cannot be offered for sale in Virginia unless the developer of the property registers with the Department of Housing and Urban Development (HUD). Registering includes filling out the appropriate paperwork, paying the appropriate fee, and annually renewing the registration.

- If an out-of-state property is registered in Virginia, this must be noted in all of the property's advertisements in Virginia.

- Out-of-state properties registered with the Board in Virginia must be offered and sold by a broker who is licensed in Virginia.

- A Virginia broker must notify the board within seven days of taking on the client if she is working for the owner/developer of an out-of-state property.

Apartment rentals in Virginia

When renting an apartment in Virginia, brokers and salespersons are required by law to supply the prospective tenant with written notification of whether or not he is required to pay a fee for services rendered. If a fee is required, the notice will also indicate how much the fee is, when it should be paid, as well as whether or not the potential tenant will receive all or some of it back if a tenancy is not established. The notification must be supplied the first time the salesperson or broker and potential tenant meet face-to-face. The notice should include the signature and date of the salesperson or broker and potential tenant, and the salesperson or broker's license number. If the potential tenant does not agree to signing the notice, the salesperson/broker must indicate this on the notice.

Three years is the period for which the salesperson/broker must keep the notice on file, and if required by the Board or other appropriate agents, it should be available upon request.

Other information that brokers should keep on file for three years are rental listings and other written notification of available apartments. This is from the date the apartment is rented. Checks, money orders, receipts, etc., should be filed for three years from the date of issuance.

All advertisements regarding an apartment available for rent should also include the statement, "The apartment advertised may no longer be available for rental."

Sherman Antitrust Act

The Sherman Antitrust Act prohibits many business practices that could unfairly restrict marketplace free competition. Some of these include:

- No price fixing

- Real estate companies cannot offer services in only particular geographical areas

- Real estate companies cannot consciously direct business away from other real estate companies

- Salespersons/brokers cannot create organizations that unfairly exclude qualified brokers from having access to marketing and sales information.

Settlement and the Conveyance of Property

Settlement procedures: Who brings/does what?

Seller:

Deed

- Current property tax certificates

- Insurance policies

- Termite inspections

- Survey maps

- Keys, garage door openers, etc.

Additional documents that the seller may have to provide when selling an income-producing property, include:

- Leases

- Operating statements

- Estoppel letters from the tenants

- Maintenance contracts

Buyer:

- Monies (good funds)

- Survey

- Insurance policy

- Flood insurance policy

- Termite certificate

The closing agent/officer:

- Ensure signatures are correctly executed

- Make sure copies are made and distributed to appropriate parties involved

- Issue checks, if applicable

- Forward the deed to be recorded

Attorneys for the buyer and seller may be present at the closing.

All applicable disclosures must be presented at closing (e.g. lead-based paint).

Before closing takes place, the majority of lenders require a termite inspection of the property, appraisal, and proof that the buyer has insurance that covers the property in the case of fire, flood, casualty, or wind damage. This is done to ensure that the property is sufficient collateral.

Purpose of closing/settlement

Before the closing takes place, the buyer and his broker (if applicable) do a final walk-through of the property to make sure it is in the condition agreed upon by the seller and buyer.

Real Estate Settlement and Procedures Act

Consumers complained about closing costs with regard to purchasing real estate as well as the procedures associated with purchasing real estate. As a result, the Real Estate Settlement and Procedures Act (RESPA) was passed.

RESPA refers to residential transactions that involve first mortgage loans made on one-four- family residences, cooperatives, and condominiums.

With RESPA, it's important to remember several key acts that are illegal:

- Fees paid for services not rendered and kickbacks are strictly prohibited under the Act.

- Also prohibited is the requirement of buyers to purchase title insurance from a specific title company.

- The amount of advance property tax and insurance payments lenders can require of borrowers must be no more than 1/6th of a year's or 2 months' worth of annual property taxes.

Deeds

The deed is the legal document used to show a transfer of ownership from the seller (grantor) to the buyer (grantee). Deeds do not have to be recorded to be valid, but if they are recorded, they are done so through the county registry of deeds. This gives a constructive notice of the transfer of ownership.

There are several different types of deeds:

Bargain and sale deed: States the consideration paid by the grantee.

Gift deed: Does not require consideration to be paid by the grantee.

Grant deed: Uses the words "I grant and convey," or similar language, and carries three implied promises: that the grantor has good title, that there are no encumbrances on the property other than those noted, and that the grantor will convey any after-acquired title to the grantee.

Quitclaim deed: Grantor conveys interest that he has in property but does not give word regarding warranty of said interest in the property.

Sheriff's deed: Transfers title of property after it has been auctioned off due to foreclosure or some other court-related action.

Tax deed: Transfers title of property sold at an auction to take care of unpaid property taxes.

There are several key elements included in the deed to make it valid. These are:

- Identification of all parties involved

- "Granting clause"

- Consideration

- Details of the rights transferred

- Legal property description

- Correct execution

- Grantor must state the deed is his "free act and deed" and notarize if the deed is to be recorded at the Land Records Department.

Torrens System

The Torrens System, also known as Land Court, is used to register land. Most land in Virginia is recorded, but some is registered. The title of registered land is searched by the Land Court. In the case of registered land, the owner is provided with a certificate of title instead of a deed.

Referencing Documents

There are two types of indexing systems, and either may be used in Virginia. These are the tract index and the alphabetical index.

For the **tract index**, each parcel of land is identified on a map. Each parcel is numbered. The number refers to a page number in a reference book. The book lists where all other documents filed for the parcel of land can be found.

The **alphabetical system**, also referred to as the **grantor-grantee index**, is a listing of all properties that changed hands during a given calendar year. To use this index, you will need the name of the buyer or seller of the piece of land you want to research. You can then use this information to find the type of document filed on the property, as well as the reference book and page number where it can be found.

Virginia Taxes

In Virginia, transfer tax is paid by both the seller and the buyer. Each party pays separately. The seller's portion of the transfer tax is known as the grantor's tax, while the buyer's portion is known as the recordation tax.

Grantor's tax in Virginia is figured as $0.50 per $500 of the value of the property, exclusive of the value of any lien or encumbrance.

Recordation tax in Virginia is figured as $0.25 per $100 of the value of the conveyance or property, whichever is greater.

Some localities in Virginia may charge an additional fee of up to one-third of the state tax.

Laws Regarding Fair Housing and Consumer Protection

Federal

Federal Civil Rights Act of 1866: Individual home sellers and real estate agencies are not allowed to racially discriminate against anyone when it comes to selling, leasing, or any other activities with real or personal property.

Federal Fair Housing Act of 1968 (Title VIII): The discrimination of individuals based on sex, race, color, religion, national origin, handicap (disability), or familial status is strictly prohibited with regard to the sale or rental of housing or vacant land.

Acts that are prohibited:

- Choosing not to sell or rent to someone who is in a protected class. Protected classes include color, race, religion/creed, ancestry/national origin, gender, disability, or familial status.

- Modifying services or conditions for different people as a way of discriminating against someone in a protected class.

- Advertising in such a way that discriminates against someone in a protected class, which would therefore prevent the sale or rental of a residence.

- Dishonestly telling an individual that a property is unavailable, as a way of discriminating against them.

- Blockbusting: Making money by encouraging homeowners to rent or sell their properties by telling them individuals of a protected class are moving into their neighborhood.

- Redlining: Changing the terms of a home loan of a person in a protected class as a way of discriminating against them.

- Preventing individuals from full participation in organizations that engage in the rental or sale of residences (e.g. multiple listing service).

- Steering: Encouraging individuals to gravitate toward or away from certain neighborhoods based on protected class.

- Stating in an appraisal report that the value of a property is impaired by any of the above prohibited activities.

- Including notes with discriminatory preferences.

- Negatively interfering with anyone who is exercising his rights.

Additional Information About Protected Classes Covered:

Familial status deals with preventing discrimination against children or families with children.

Discriminating against disabled (mentally or physically) persons by not making reasonable accommodations regarding policies or necessary changes to the premises is prohibited.

Since 1991, homes that are four-family or larger are required to be disability accessible for first- floor units. In homes where elevators are present, units on upper floors must also be disability accessible.

The 1968 Federal Fair Housing Act covers residential property.

What does Title VIII Not Cover?

- The sale or rental by an individual who owns three or fewer properties and does not use a broker, and does not engage in discriminatory advertising, and has not sold another property in the last two years.

- The rental of rooms in an owner-occupied, multi-family home with two to four units, providing no salesperson is used and he has not engaged in discriminatory advertising.

- The sale or rental of a property by a religious organization to a person of the same religion (for non-commercial purposes), providing no prohibited restrictions are enforced.

- The rental of properties managed by a private club for members for purposes other than commercial.

- Elderly housing that meets particular HUD rules.

Individuals who believe they have been discriminated against can file a complaint with HUD or take civil action with the court.

If it is proven that the individuals have indeed been discriminated against, the offender may face penalties such as civil penalties, monetary fines, and court costs, among other things.

Virginia State General Law

Virginia Fair Housing Law

In Virginia, there are two protected class categories: 1. Based on race, color, religion, national origin, ancestry, sex, elderliness, or disability and 2. Familial status (presence of children under 18 years of age).

Category 1

There are some exemptions to this law regarding home sellers, but not real estate agencies. These exemptions become void if discriminatory advertising has taken place. The exemptions:

- When an owner-occupied, two-family residence is being leased

- If the housing is designated "elderly housing" and it receives state or federal funding, it is exempt based only on age.

- If a community is an authorized "55+" community and is situated on at least 10 acres, it is exempt based only on age.

Category 2

Not agreeing to rent or sell to someone solely because they have children is illegal. This also includes not renting to someone with children because the owner knows the property has lead paint or other safety violations they are not willing to get up to code. Discrimination in advertising is never allowed, nor is advertising that is different for people with or without children. As with Category 1 under the Virginia Fair Housing Act, there are exemptions to this rule:

- If the residence is a three-family or smaller residence and there is an elderly or ill resident for whom allowing children to live on the premises would be a hardship.

- The lease is a temporary owner/occupant lease.

- The lease is for an owner-occupied two-family residence.

It is also a violation of fair housing standards to refuse credit services or rental accommodations to someone solely because he or she receives public assistance, rental assistance, or housing subsidy.

Individuals in one of these categories who feel they have been discriminated against can file a complaint with the Virginia Commission on Equal Opportunity or take civil action with the court.

If it is proven that the individuals have indeed been discriminated against, they can be compensated in a variety of ways such as affirmative relief or civil penalties.

If it is determined that a real estate agent is in violation of this law, he may have his license suspended or revoked.

Virginia Uniform Deceptive Trade Practices Act (UDTPA)

This law applies to salespeople and brokers and forbids deceptive and unfair trade practices. Violation of the law can result in being sued for a maximum of triple damages and attorney's fees.

Lead Paint Law

There is federal and state law that real estate agents must abide by regarding lead paint disclosure requirements. For homes built before 1978, the prospective buyer must be provided with a Department of Public Health Property Transfer Notification Certification that informs the buyer of whether or not the seller is aware of lead paint anywhere on the property. The seller must provide reports about it. The buyer then has 10 days to have a test completed to check for lead paint. This process is done before the prospective buyer signs a Purchase and Sale Agreement.

If the prospective buyer decides he would like to continue with the purchase, he must be given a Lead Paint Notification and Tenant Certificate Form. Also, if the new tenant has a child under the age of six who lives in the property, the current owner must de-lead.

Additionally, potential hazards such as those regarding smoke detectors must also be addressed. Within 60 days of closing on the property, the fire department must inspect and issue a smoke detector certificate saying the smoke detectors in the property are sufficient and properly working. Homes that are three-family or larger must also have hard-wired smoke detectors in common areas of the home. Homes that are six-family or larger must have hard-wired smoke detectors everywhere in the property.

Management of Property

Condominiums

Condominiums in Virginia are governed by the Virginia Condominium Act. Units can be owned by an individual fee simple estate, which means in the case of payment default, only that individual owner is penalized, not all other owners.

The condominium master deed explains details of the property, each unit, and land and common area percentage ownership for each buyer. In addition to the master deed, a unit deed also exists. A unit deed is provided each time the sale of a unit takes place. The unit deed includes bylaws, by which each owner agrees to follow. The bylaws describe the condominium association and its legal authority.

There are typically fees associated with condominium ownership that are paid monthly. The amount due depends on the percentage of ownership for each owner.

Common areas of the condominium are for the use of all owners, unless designated as a limited common element (e.g. balcony).

The transfer of ownership of a condominium in Virginia must follow this process: (1) The current owner must obtain a certified letter from the condominium association. This document states that all condominium fees have been paid through the end of that current month. (2) The current owner must obtain an insurance certificate that proves that the new owner and his mortgage holder will be protected by the condominium master insurance policy.

Cooperatives

Cooperatives are unlike condominiums in they have one owner, a corporation. There is a blanket mortgage on the property. The corporation is responsible for paying *ad valorem* taxes.

The buyers of each coop unit are considered stockholders, as once they make the purchase, they are given a stock certificate in the corporation. With ownership, the buyer has a "proprietary unit lease" which means they can occupy their unit for the life of the corporation.

The downside to ownership in a cooperative as opposed to a condominium is that if one shareholder defaults on his monthly payment, the other shareholder tenants are affected and they must come together to make up any shortfall.

Time Sharing

Time sharing is just as its name states. Several owners share interest in one condominium unit with the right to occupy the property for a certain amount of time each year. All owners pay costs such as maintenance and management fees. The amounts depend on the ownership period and total number of available ownership periods. Time share ownership can be fee simple or lease-hold interest. Another option with time shares is an exchange program, where owners can exchange their time share credits for the occupancy of other locations.

Subdivisions

"Subdivision" is the term used to describe large tracts of land that are divided into smaller parcels that will then be for sale. The land is improved (added infrastructure, etc.) and typically regulated by local, state, and federal law. The plat will be recorded, showing lots, blocks, etc.

If the subdivision includes more than 25 lots, exceeding 20 acres and is offered for sale, crossing state lines, HUD (Federal Interstate Land Sales Full Disclosure Act) requires that several reports be filed.

Real Estate Math

The Real Estate Math section of this guide should not be taken lightly. Most state exams include around 10% math questions, but you don't have to be a mathematician to complete this part effectively. Use this review to refresh your understanding of and learn arithmetic, algebra, geometry, and word problems. You will also have the opportunity to practice with the included sample problems for each math topic.

Some of the math question types you may come across on your exam include:

- Area
- Percents
- Property tax
- Loan-to-Value Ratios
- Points
- Equity
- Qualifying Buyers
- Prorations
- Commissions
- Proceeds from sales
- Transfer Tax/Conveyance Tax/Revenue Stamps
- Competitive Market Analyses
- Income Properties
- Depreciation

Use the following to help you complete the math questions.

Tips for Completing Math Questions

Before taking the exam, and especially while you are completing the math portion of the exam, there are a few things you may want to keep in mind:

Leave No Question Unanswered

Although you may not know the answer to every question right off the top of your head, it is advisable that you answer every question to the best of your ability. You immediately have a one in four chance of getting the answer correct. There are also some instances where an answer choice is clearly not correct, which betters your chance for selecting the right answer.

Use a Calculator

In some states you are allowed to use calculator; check with the testing center first. However, you shouldn't rely solely on the calculator as this can slow you down, but using it to work out some mathematical equations can prove to be very helpful.

Utilize Scrap Paper

Let nothing take the place of scrap paper. While using a calculator can help you get the answer quickly, writing down your thought process provides information for you to refer to in case you get stuck.

Review! Review! Review!

Avoiding an incorrect answer can be something as simple as checking your work.

Math Review

Basic math skills in the areas of arithmetic, algebra, geometry, and word problems will be necessary. Here's a review.

Arithmetic

Multiplication

"Factor" is the term used to describe numbers that are being multiplied. The answer is known as the "product."

Example:

2 x 5 = 10   2 and 5 are the factors. 10 is the product.

A multiplication problem can be presented in a variety of ways.

- You may see a dot between two factors, which denotes multiplication:
  $2 \cdot 5 = 10$

- The use of parentheses around one or more factors denotes multiplication:
  (2)5 = 10

  2(5) = 10

  (2)(5) = 10

- A number next to a variable denotes multiplication:
  2a = 10

  Multiply "2" and "a" to arrive at the product of 10.

Division

The "divisor" is the number divided by; while the "dividend" is the number the divisor is going into. The result is the quotient.

Division is similar to multiplication in that there are several ways to indicate the operation.

12÷3 = 4

12/3 = 4

$\frac{12}{3}$ = 4

Decimals

The key to understanding decimals is knowing each place value.

Here is a table to help you remember:

4	6	3	2	6	.	5	7	9	1
Ten Thousands	Thousands	Hundreds	Tens	Ones	Decimal	Tenths	Hundredths	Thousandths	Ten Thousandths

Using the above table, this number would be expressed as: 46,326.5791

It is also important to understand how to round decimals. If the number immediately following the number you must round is 5 or greater, you increase the preceding number by 1. If the number immediately following the number you must round is less than 5, drop that number and leave the preceding number as is.

Example:

0.236 would be rounded to 0.24

0.234 would be rounded to 0.23

Adding Fractions

Adding fractions with the same denominators is a simple operation. You add the numerators together and leave the denominator as it appears.

Example:

$$\frac{3}{5} + \frac{1}{5} = \frac{4}{5}$$

Adding fractions with different denominators requires you to find the least common denominator. The least common denominator is the smallest number that each of your denominators can divide into evenly.

Example:

$\frac{4}{6} + \frac{3}{4}$ The least common denominator is 12 because 6 x 2 = 12 and 4 x 3 = 12.

Once you have determined the least common denominator, each fraction should be converted to its new form. This is done by multiplying the numerator and denominator in each fraction by the appropriate number in order to arrive at the least common denominator. Next, you add the new numerators, which gives you the final answer.

Example:

$$\frac{4}{6} + \frac{3}{4} = \frac{2(4)}{2(6)} + \frac{3(3)}{3(4)} = \frac{8}{12} + \frac{9}{12} = \frac{17}{12}$$

Subtracting Fractions

Subtracting fractions with the same denominators is a simple operation. You subtract the numerators and leave the denominator as it appears.

Example:

$$\frac{3}{5} - \frac{1}{5} = \frac{2}{5}$$

Subtracting fractions with different denominators requires you to find the least common denominator. The least common denominator is the smallest number that each of your denominators can divide into evenly.

Example:

$\frac{8}{9} - \frac{3}{6}$ The least-common denominator is 18 because 9 x 2 = 18 and 6 x 3 = 18.

Once you have determined the least common denominator, each fraction should be converted to its new form. This is done by multiplying the numerator and denominator in each fraction by the appropriate number in order to arrive at the least common denominator. Next, you subtract the new numerators, which gives you the final answer.

Example:

$$\frac{8}{9} - \frac{3}{6} = \frac{2(8)}{2(9)} - \frac{3(3)}{3(6)} = \frac{16}{18} - \frac{9}{18} = \frac{7}{18}$$

Multiplying Fractions

When multiplying fractions, the denominators of the fractions can be the same or different. Either way, the operation is performed the same.

Multiply the numerators together and multiply the denominators together.

Example:

$$\frac{4}{7} \times \frac{3}{5} = \frac{12}{35} \quad (4 \times 3) / (7 \times 5) = \frac{12}{35}$$

Dividing Fractions

When dividing fractions, you actually multiply the first fraction by the reciprocal of the second fraction.

You find the reciprocal of a number by turning it upside down. For example, the reciprocal of $\frac{3}{8}$ is $\frac{8}{3}$.

Solve the problem.

$$\frac{18}{24} \div \frac{2}{4} = \frac{18}{24} \times \frac{4}{2} = \frac{72}{48} = \frac{3}{2}$$

Percent

"Percent" is used to describe a portion of a whole, with the whole being 100.

How do I change a decimal to a percentage?

This operation is simple. Move the decimal two places to the right, and add a percentage sign.

Example:

.32 = 32%

.04 = 4%

.1 = 10%

.102 = 10.2%

How do I change a fraction to a percentage?

The first step in converting a fraction to a percentage is to change the fraction to a decimal. Do so by dividing the denominator into the numerator. From here you move the decimal two places to the right of the number, and then add the percentage sign.

Example:

$^3/_6$ = .5 = 50%

$^1/_4$ = .25 = 25%

1/8 = .125 = 12.5%

How do I change a percentage to a decimal?

Simply slide the decimal two places to the left and take away the percentage symbol.

Example:

69% = .69

4% = .04

125% = 1.25

How do I change a percentage to a fraction?

Divide the number by 100. Reduce to lowest terms.

Example:

$25\% = {}^{25}/_{100} = {}^{1}/_{4}$

$62\% = {}^{62}/_{100} = {}^{31}/_{50}$

$125\% = {}^{125}/_{50} = 1\,{}^{1}/_{4}$

How do I change a percentage that is greater than 100 to a decimal or mixed fraction?

To change to a decimal:

Move the decimal point two places to the left and drop the percent sign.

$298\% = 2.98$

$600\% = 6.0$

$980\% = 9.8$

To change to a mixed fraction –

$275\% = {}^{275}/_{100} = {}^{200}/_{100} + {}^{75}/_{100} = 2 + {}^{3}/_{4} = 2\,{}^{3}/_{4}$

$275\% = 2\,{}^{3}/_{4}$

$550\% = {}^{550}/_{100} = {}^{500}/_{100} + {}^{50}/_{100} = 5 + {}^{1}/_{2} = 5\,{}^{1}/_{2}$

$550\% = 5\,{}^{1}/_{2}$

Conversions Commonly Seen in Real Estate:

Fraction	Decimal	Percentage
½	.5	50%
¼	.25	25%
1/3	.333...	33.3...%
2/3	.666...	66.6...%
1/10	.1	10%
1/8	.125	12.5%
1/6	.1666...	16.6...%
1/5	.2	20%

Algebra

Equations

To solve an equation, you must determine what is equal to the unidentified variable.

Things to remember about equations:

- There are two parts to an equation. They are separated by an equal sign.
- An operation performed on an equation must be done to each part.
- When beginning to solve the equation, priority #1 is to get the variables on one side and the known numbers on the other.
- You will sometimes have to divide both parts of the equation using the same divisor. This will enable the variable to equal an exact number.

How do I check an equation to make sure it is correct?

Once you've solved the equation, take the number equal to the variable and input into the original equation.

Example:

x = 5

Original equation: $\frac{1}{x\,(2)} = \frac{x-4}{10}$

$\frac{1}{5(2)} = \frac{5-4}{10}$

$\frac{1}{10} = \frac{1}{10}$

x = 5

Algebraic Fractions

Example:

How do I subtract two fractions with different denominators?

$\frac{x}{4} - \frac{x}{8}$

$\frac{x}{4} - \frac{x}{8} = \frac{x\,(2)}{4\,(2)} - \frac{x}{8}$

$\frac{2x}{8} - \frac{x}{8} = \frac{x}{8}$

Geometry

Terms to remember:

- **Area** – Refers to the space inside a two-dimensional figure.
- **Circumference** – Refers to the distance around the edge of a circle.
- **Perimeter** – Refers to the total distance around a two-dimensional figure.
- **Radius** – Refers to the distance from the center point of a circle to its perimeter.

Area

Area refers to the space inside a two-dimensional figure.

In the triangle below, the area is the part that is shaded green.

 = **Area**

Area Formulas for Various Shapes

Circle: $A = \pi r^2$

Sphere: $A = 4\pi r^2$

Rectangle: $A = lw$

Square: $A = s^2$

Triangle: $A = bh$

Parallelogram: $A = bh$

What do the above letters/symbols mean?

A: Area

π: "pi" 3.14

r: Radius

l: Length

w: Width

s: Side length

b: Base

h: Height

Examples of area:

Area of circle

Area of rectangle

$A = \pi r^2$

$A = \pi \times (5 \times 5)$

$A = \pi \times 25$

$A = 3.14 \times 25$

$A = 78.54$

$A = lw$

$A = 8 \text{ mm} \times 3 \text{ mm} = 24 \text{ mm}^2$

Perimeter

Perimeter refers to the total distance around a two-dimensional figure.

It is calculated simply by adding together all of the sides of the figure.

Example:

5

7   7

         3

Perimeter = 7 + 7 + 5 + 3 = 22

Circumference is the perimeter of a circle.

Formula for circumference: $C = 2\pi r$

Word Problems

Understanding word problems is crucial to doing well on the math problems of the Real Estate Exam, as these make up a significant portion of the math problems found on the exam.

Before knowing how to solve the problems, you must understand what the problem is asking.

Terms you will commonly see:

- **Increase**
  What operation do you perform?

  Answer: Addition

  Example:

  A number is increased by 7, which means x + 7.

- **Less than**
  What operation do you perform?

  Answer: Subtraction

Example:

A number is less than 12 by x, which means $12 - x$.

- **Product or times**
  What operation do you perform?

  Answer: Multiplication

  Example:

  A number times 8, which means $x(8)$.

- **Times the sum of**
  What operation do you perform?

  Answer: Multiply a number by a quantity

  Example:

  Six times the sum of nine and a number, which is $6(9 + x)$.

- **Of**
  What operation do you perform?

  Answer: Multiplication

  Example:

5% of 100 is 5, which means 5% x 100 = 5.

- **Is**
  What operation do you perform?

  Answer: Equals

  Example:

  10 is 20 minus 10, which means 10 = 20 − 10.

- **The use of two variables**
  What operation do you perform?

  Answer: Whatever the equation states

  Example:

  A number y exceeds 3 times a number x by 8, which means $y = 3x + 8$.

Creating and Using Variables in Word Problems

In order to solve some word problems, you may be required to create and use variables. The first step in doing so is to determine what you know and don't know regarding the equation.

Examples:

Perry made 5 more dollars than Billy on his paper route.

What do you know? Perry made $5 more

What don't you know? The amount that Billy made

So,

The amount Billy made is x and the amount Perry made is x + 5.

Pam made 3 times as many A's on her report card as Jan.

What do you know? Pam made 3 times as many A's as Jan

What don't you know? The number of A's that Jan made

So,

The number of A's Jan made is x and the number of A's Pam made is 3x.

Greg has 4 more than 2 times the number of marbles that Shelly has.

What do you know? Greg has 4 more than 2 times the number of marbles Shelly has

What don't you know? The number of marbles Shelly has

So,

The number of marbles Shelly has is x and the number of marbles Greg has 2x + 4.

Percentage Word Problems

There are three main types of percentage word problems. All three types follow the same formula for calculating the result.

Formula:

$$\frac{\#}{\text{part}} \quad \frac{\%}{\text{whole}} = \frac{}{100}$$

Calculate the problem substituting the appropriate information in the above formula.

Keep this in mind:

- On the percentage side, 100 will always be in the denominator.
- If you are not provided with a percentage amount to use as the numerator, use a variable.
- On the number side, the number always equals the whole (100%). In the word problem, this number follows the term "of".
- On the number side, the numerator is the number that's equal to the percent.

Examples:

How do you find the percentage when you know the number?

What is the number that is equal to 40% of 95?

$$\overset{\#}{} \quad \overset{\%}{}$$

$$\frac{x}{95} = \frac{40}{100}$$

Cross multiply:

$100(x) = 40(95)$

$100x = 3800$

$x = 3800/100$

x = 38

Answer: 38 is 40% of 95

How do you find the number when you know the percentage?

40% of what number is 38?

$$\#\qquad\%$$

$$\frac{38}{x} \ = \ \frac{40}{100}$$

Cross multiply:

100(38) = 40(x)

3800 = 40x

$$\frac{3800}{40} \ = \ \frac{40x}{40}$$

95 = x

Answer: 38 is 40% of 95

How do you find what percentage one number is of another?

What percentage of 95 is 38?

$$\#\qquad\%$$

$$^{38}/_{95} = \ ^{x}/_{100}$$

Cross multiply:

100(38) = 95(x)

$$3800 = 95x$$

$$\frac{3800}{95} = \frac{95x}{95}$$

$$40 = x$$

Answer: 38 is 40% of 95

Calculating Rate

Calculating cost per unit, interest rate, and tax rate are common problems found on the real estate exam. The purpose of rate is to compare two amounts, using various units of measure.

Rate formula:

Calculating cost per unit

Example:

How much do 2 square feet cost if 250 square feet cost $2,500?

Answer:

$$\frac{2,500}{250} = \$10 \text{ / square foot}$$

Therefore, 2 square feet cost $20

Interest rate

The formula for simple interest is:

Interest = principal x rate x time or I = (PRT)

Equivalencies

Here are a few measurement equivalencies that will help you:

- 1 foot (ft.') = 12 inches (in.")
- 1 yard (yd.) = 3 ft. or 36 in.
- 1 mile = 5,280 ft.
- 1 mile = 1,760 yards
- 1 square foot (sq. ft., ft.^{2}) = 144 square inches (sq. in., in.^{2})
- 1 square yard = 9 square feet
- 1 acre = 43,560
- 1 square mile = 640 acres

Basic Percentage

Determining basic percentage.

Example:

How do you calculate 53% of $3,645?

Answer:

Convert 53% to a decimal by moving the decimal two places to the left.

53% = .53

Multiply the result by $3,645.

(.53) ($3,645) = $1,931.85

$1,931.85 is 53% of $3,645.

Percentage: Interest

How do you calculate the rate of interest being charged?

Example:

Paul Billings borrowed $22,000. He is paying $1,200 / year in interest. What is the interest rate he is being charged?

interest = principal x rate x time

The principal amount is $22,000

The interest amount is $1,200

Rate = Let the unknown interest rate be i

Time = 1 year

Using the formula, Interest = principal x rate (i) x time, solve for x.

$1,200 = 22,000(i)(1)$

$1,200 = 22,000i$

$$\frac{1,200}{22,000} = \frac{i}{22,000}$$

$.055 = i$

Convert the decimal to a percent. Do this by moving the decimal two places to the right.

$.055 = 5.5\%$

Area of Various Figures

Rectangles

Keep in mind: The formula for area in a rectangle is: Area = (length) (width)

Example:

Theresa purchased two small lots of land. One is 70 feet by 20 feet and the other, 80 feet by 30 feet. What is the total square feet of land that she has?

Answer:

$A = (70) (20) + (80) (30) =$

$A = 1400 + 2400 = 3,800$ square feet

Theresa has a total of 3,800 square feet of land.

How do you find the length of a rectangle if you only know the area and width?

Keep in mind: The formula for area in a rectangle is: Area = (length) (width)

Example:

Theresa has 2,400 square feet of land that is 30 feet in width. What is the length of the land?

Answer:

2,400 = (x) (30)

$^{2,400}/_{30}$ = $^{(x)(30)}/_{30}$

x = $^{2400}/_{30}$

x = 80 feet

Triangles

Keep in mind: The formula for area in a triangle is: Area = ½ bh

Example:

For their small business, Paul and Sally Green are buying a triangular piece of land. The base of the property is 150 feet. The side that is perpendicular to the base is also 150 feet. What is the total number of square feet for the property?

Area = x

Base = 150

Height = 150

x = (½ or .5) (150) (150)

x = (½ or .5) (22,500)

x = 11,250 square feet

Circles

Keep in mind: The formula for area in a circle is: A = πr^2

Example:

Gill is using a circular cover over a circular piece of land for a special project. The radius of the circular land area is 23 feet. What is the area of the cover over it?

For "π," use 3.14.

What do you know?

Radius = 23

π = 3.14

Area = x

Solve.

$A = \pi r^2$

A = (3.14)(23)(23) = 1,661.06 square feet

The area of the cover is 1,661.06 square feet.

Property Tax

Property tax questions are solved using percentages and rates.

Example:

Laurie Collins lives in Purple County. The tax rate for Purple County is $5.89 per one hundred of assessed valuation. Ms. Collins shares that she pays $2,550 in taxes. What is her property assessment? Round answer to nearest 10 cents.

What do you know?

Taxes = $2,550

Tax rate = $5.89 per hundred (%)

Assessment = x

$5.89 is 5.89%. Convert the percentage to a decimal: .0589

.0589 of the assessed value of the house is $2,550, which means:

(.0589) (x) = 2,550

Solve.

$$^{(.0589)(x)}/_{.0589} = {}^{(2,550)}/_{.0589}$$

x = $43,293.718

Rounded to the nearest 10 cents, the answer is $43,293.70.

How do you determine the tax rate if you know the amount of taxes paid and assessment amount?

Example:

Mrs. Ferguson said her taxes are $1,300 and property assessment $40,000. What is the tax rate percentage?

What do you know?

Taxes = $1,300

Assessment = $40,000

Rate (%) = x

In equation form, this means:

($40,000) (x) = 1,300

Solve.

$$^{40,000 \, x}/_{40,000} = {}^{1,300}/_{40,000}$$

x = .0325

Convert to a percentage.

The rate is 3.25%

Loan-to-Value Ratios (LTV)

Problems regarding Loan-to-Value ratios typically involve percentages.

A mortgage loan that bears interest at 25% per annum is at an 85% LTV. The interest on the original balance for year one is $21,474. When securing the loan, what was the value of the property? Round to the nearest dollar.

Solve.

Step #1: Determine the loan amount.

What do you know?

25% of the loan amount is $21,474.

Loan amount = x

In equation form this means:

($21,474) = (25%) (x) or ($21,474) = (.25) (x)

21,474/ .25 =

x = $85,896

The loan amount is $85,896

Step #2: Determine the value of the property.

What do you know?

Loan amount = $85,896

Loan-to-value ratio = 85%

Value = x

$85,896 is 85% of the value

In equation form this means:

(85% or .85) (x) = $85,896

$$^{.85x}/_{.85} = {}^{85,896}/_{.85}$$

x = $101,054.118

The value amount is $101,054

Points

"Point" is the term used to describe loan discounts. Each point represents one percent of the face amount of the loan. For example, 3 points means 3% of the face amount of the loan.

Example:

Burt is attempting to obtain an $80,000 FHA mortgage loan. In order to do so, he must pay a 2-point discount (2%). What is the discount amount?

Answer:

Before solving the problem, convert the percentage to a decimal.

2% = .02

What do you know?

Amount of the loan = $80,000

Points = .02

Amount of the discount = x

x = (.02) (80,000)

x = $1,600

Equity

How do you calculate the value of a home?

Example:

John owns a home on which he has three mortgages. The first mortgage balance is $190,000. The second mortgage balance is $20,000 and third mortgage balance, $10,000. The equity in John's home is $50,000. What is the value of John's home?

In this problem, the value of the home is the total of all three mortgages plus the equity.

Answer:

$190,000 + $20,000 + $10,000 + $50,000 = $270,000

The value of the home is $270,000.

Qualifying Buyers

Megan is attempting to qualify for an FHA loan to buy a home. Her ratio requirement is 34/41. She makes $75,000/year and has a $900 monthly car payment. What is her maximum PITI payment?

Answer:

First, divide Megan's annual income by the number of months in a year (12).

$75,000/12 = $6,250

Megan's monthly income is $6,250

Next, determine the front-end qualifier by multiplying Megan's monthly income by the front-end portion (in decimal form) of the ratio.

$6,250 (.34) = $2,125

$2,125 is the front-end qualifier

Lastly, determine the back-end qualifier by multiplying Megan's monthly income by the back-end portion (in decimal form) of the ratio. Then subtract Megan's debt amount from this number.

$6,250 (.41) = $2,562.50 - $900 = $1,662.50

$1,662.50 is the back-end qualifier

The maximum PITI is $1,662.50. The maximum PITI is the lower of the two qualifiers.

Prorations

During settlement, there is typically a reconciliation that needs to take place regarding money that is owed as of the settlement date. The best way to remember who owes what is by remembering the simple fact that he who uses the service is the one who has to pay for it. When calculating these figures, unless otherwise noted, you may always use a 30-day month and 360-day calendar year.

Example:

Mr. Perkins paid his 2012 calendar year property taxes in the amount of $2,400 one year in advance. He sells his house to Mr. Dickinson in April 2012 and settles in May of that same year. With regard to the amount paid in taxes for 2012, how much do the two parties owe each other?

What do you know?

	Mr. Perkins	Mr. Dickinson
How many months paid for?	12 ($2,400)	0 ($0)
How many months used/will use?	4 ($800)	8 ($1,600)
How many months should he be reimbursed for?		
	8 ($1,600)	0 ($0)
How many months should he reimbursed for?		
	0 ($0)	8 ($1,600)

Mr. Dickinson should be debited $1,600. Mr. Perkins should be credited $1,600.

Commissions

Commission calculation problems are common. They usually seek to determine a percentage, but they may also ask for a dollar amount.

Example:

The broker made her first home sale for $127,000. The total amount of commission is $7,700. What is the broker's commission rate?

Answer:

What do you know?

Home price: $127,000

Commission: $7,700

Commission rate: x

In equation form, this means:

$127,000 \, x = 7,700$

Solve.

$x = 7,700/127,000$

$x = 0.060$

Change to a decimal and round to the nearest whole percent.

$0.060 = 6\%$

Example:

An agent made a 6% commission on the sale of a home. The sale price was $345,867. The agent made another 6% commission on the sale of a $243,542 home. What is the total dollar amount the agent received in commission on the two homes?

Determine the commission amount on the first home sale.

$345,867 \, (.06) = \$20,752.02$

Determine the commission amount on the second home sale.

$243,542 \, (.06) = \$14,612.52$

Add together the two commission amounts.

$20,752.02 + $14,612.52 = $35,364.54

Total commission = $35,364.54

Sale Proceeds

Example:

The agent is working with the homeowner to determine the list price for the homeowner's home in order to meet the homeowner's desire to net at least $30,000. The current mortgage balance is $235,000 and commission to take into consideration is 7%. If they list and sell the property at $300,000, would the homeowner net at least $30,000?

What do you know?

Expenses: Total - $256,000

> Mortgage balance: $235,000

> Commission: $21,000

Sale price: $300,000

$235,000 + $21,000 = $256,000

$300,000 - $256,000 = $44,000

The homeowner would net $44,000. Therefore, he would net at least $30,000.

Transfer Tax/Conveyance Tax/Revenue Stamps

In Virginia, buyers pay a recordation tax, which is figured at $0.25 per $100 of the conveyance or value of the property, whichever is greater.

Sellers pay a grantor's tax, which is figured as $0.50 per $500 of the value of the property, exclusive of the value of any lien or encumbrance. Certain localities may charge an additional fee.

Recordation Tax (Virginia) Example:

A homeowner sells her house for $432,000. How much does the buyer owe the state in recordation tax?

There are 4,320 ($100s) in $432,000. Therefore, you multiply the tax amount per $100, which is $0.25 times 4,320.

$0.25 x 4320 = $1,080

The recordation tax amount for the sale of a $432,000 home is $1,080.

Competitive Market Analyses (CMA)

CMAs help sellers get a better understanding of the market value of their property, which could in turn help them decide on the sale price. Although very useful, it is important to note that CMAs are not appraisals.

CMA problems are solved by using measurable aspects of comparable properties to come to a specific value.

Example:

Mr. Stone has the blueprint for two homes he would like to build. Home A is 62' x 94' in size and will cost $234,985 to build. Home B is 90' x 112' in size. If each house costs the same per square foot to build, how much will it cost to build Home B?

Answer:

Remember, the formula to find Area for a rectangle is: A = lw.

Area of Home A: 62(94) = 5,828 square feet

Area of Home B: 90(112) = 10,080 square feet

Cost to build Home A / square foot: $\dfrac{\$234,985}{5,828}$ = $40.32

Cost to build Home B = 10,080($40.32) = $406,425.60

Income Properties

Example:

Bob, a local real estate investor is interested in buying an income property that creates gross income in the amount of $270,500. He discovers that the operating costs of this property will equal 65% of the gross income. Ideally, he would like to acquire a 15% return. With his desire to have a 15% return, what is the most he can pay for the property?

Answer:

What do you know?

Gross income= $270,500

Operating costs= 65% of $270,500

Net income = Gross income – operating costs

Desired return= 15%

Most the investor can pay = x

Step #1:

Determine the dollar amount of the operating costs. Start off by converting the percentage to a decimal.

65% = .65

Operating costs = (.65)(270,500) = $175,825

Step #2:

Gross income – Operating costs = Net income

$270,500 - $175,825 = $94,675

Step #3:

The investor wants his net income to be 15% of what he pays for the property. Convert the percent to a decimal, and then determine the most he can pay.

15% = .15

$94,675 = (.15)(x)

$$\frac{\$94,675}{.15} = \frac{(.15)(x)}{.15}$$

$$\frac{\$94,675}{.15} = x$$

$631,167 (Rounded to the nearest dollar)

Depreciation

You may encounter "depreciation" problems on the exam, but those representing the straight-line method are the only ones you will probably see.

The formula for the straight-line method of depreciation:

$$\frac{replacement\ cost}{years\ of\ useful\ life} = \text{annual depreciation}$$

If the depreciation rate is not given, you can calculate it dividing the total depreciation, which is 100%, by the useful life of the building.

For example, if a building has 25 years of useful life, then you will use this calculation:

$$\frac{100\%}{25} = 4\%$$

This means that the building has an annual depreciation rate of 4%.

Example:

It has been determined that the replacement cost of a 15 year old building is $90,000. Since it has 35 years of useful life left, how much can be charged to annual depreciation?

What do you know?

Replacement cost = $90,000

Useful life = 35 years

Using the formula $\frac{replacement\ cost}{years\ of\ useful\ life} = $ annual depreciation, calculate annual depreciation.

$$\frac{\$90,000}{35} = \$2571 \text{ (Rounded to the nearest dollar)}$$

Example:

The annual depreciation of a building is $3245. What is the total depreciation of a 19 year old building?

annual depreciation x age of building = total depreciation

$3245 x 19 = $61,655

Total depreciation = $61,655

Example:

The replacement cost of a building is $62,000. The total depreciation of said building is $19,354. What is the current value of the building?

replacement cost – depreciation = current value

$62,000 - $19,354 = $42,646

Current value of the building = $42,646

Summary

It is our hope that this Real Estate Math review has helped reinforce your knowledge of the topics you will most likely see on the math section of the Real Estate Exam. For those of you who feel like you could use a bit more of a refresher, feel free to take the included practice exams over and over until you feel confident that you can triumphantly complete the Real Estate Exam. Good luck!

Real Estate Glossary

>A

abandonment giving up the right to possess a property, building or real estate area through non-use and intention.

abstract of title the background of a property listing legal transactions and information.

abutting sitting next to another property.

acceleration clause an addendum that forces the borrower to repay the entire loan upon the lender's insistence for specific reasons listed in the clause.

acceptance agreement to an offer.

accretion increase of the amount of land by natural deposits of soil on onto the property.

accrued depreciation the total loss of value on the property.

accrued items the additional costs still outstanding at the close of the real estate deal, such as interest, insurance, HOA fees or taxes.

acknowledgement agreement to fulfill admitted responsibility.

acre a section of land that is 4,840 square yards or 43,560 square feet in area.

actual eviction a step-by-step procedure to remove renters from property.

actual notice specific information given to a party, such as a tenant, landlord, buyer or seller.

addendum a clause that provides more specific information to clarify a contract.

adjacent property or buildings next to each other but might not touch each other.

adjoining property or buildings next to each other that do touch each other.

adjustable rate mortgage (ARM) a loan rate that changes throughout the period of the loan. Sometimes called a variable rate or flexible rate.

adjusted basis the final cost of a property after improvements are added and deductions or reduced value are subtracted.

adjustment date the date agreed upon by the buyer and seller for financial changes.

administrator a court-appointed individual who executes a person's estate if there is not a will.

ad valorem tax property tax on the current value of the land.

adverse possession the ways by which a person may acquire property, such as through purchase, inheritance or other methods, including without payment as in a squatter.

adverse selection principal is not able to determine if an agent has accurately represented his or her ability.

affidavit a sworn promise before a person in authority.

agency a professional company that can act on behalf of another, such as a real estate agency or a title agency.

agency theory addresses conflicts of interest between agents and principals.

agent a professional individual who can act on behalf of another, such as a real estate agent or a title agent.

agreement of sale a contract between two parties to buy/sell property, usually over time.

air rights the right to air space above a property, separate from the property land itself.

alienation placement of ownership of property from one person/company to another person/company.

alienation clause an addendum to the mortgage contract that keeps the borrower from reselling the property without paying the lender.

allodial system a national system overseen by law that monitors property ownership.

amenities "extras" on a property that make it worth more or more attractive to buyers. Location or kitchen upgrades are two examples of amenities.

amortization paying off the principal and interest on a debt with equal payments until the debt is repaid.

amortization schedule the time frame set up over which the principal and interest of the debt is repaid.

amortize to pay off the principal and interest on a loan.

annual percentage rate (APR) the percentage above the principal added onto the loan over 12 months. It includes additional costs, such as closing costs and fees, and not just interest rates.

anti-deficiency law a statute that stops the lender from pursuing the buyer for a loss on a property after a foreclosure sale.

antitrust laws national laws that encourage free market trade and practices and prohibit the restriction of such.

apportionments the division of costs, such as fees and HOA responsibilities, between the seller and purchaser.

appraisal assessing the worth of land or property by a professional, qualified person who is usually licensed.

appraised value the worth of the land or property as determined by the licensed professional.

appraiser a professional, qualified person so licensed by the state to determine the value of land or property.

appreciation growth in the worth of real estate.

appurtenance an attachment to land or edifices that now conveys with the property.

arbitration dispute resolution through the use of a third party.

ARELLO an online company that encourages the cooperation of decision makers in the real estate business.

assessed value the tax-related value put on a property.

assessment the placement of tax-related value on a property.

assessor a professional who determines the tax-related value of a property.

asset something of value that belongs to a person, such as cash, property, bonds, etc.

assignment the transfer of a mortgage from one agency to another.

assumption of mortgage the process of the buyer taking over the seller's mortgage.

attachment placing a legal hold on a property to pay for a judgment.

attest to agree to the truth of a document by signing it.

attorney-in-fact a person who acts as a legal representative for another; does not need to be a professional lawyer.

avulsion transfer of land because water, such as a stream or brook, changes course.

>B

balloon mortgage a mortgage with small payments due for a specified period, such as three to five years, with a lump sum or balloon due at the end of the mortgage.

balloon payment the lump payment at the end of a balloon mortgage.

bankruptcy the legal discharge of most debts through the courts.

bargain and sale deed a document transferring property from seller to buyer without guaranteeing the validity of the transfer.

baseline a line in surveying that runs east to west and acts a point of reference for corresponding lines that run north to south.

benchmark a fixed point of reference by which elevation is marked.

beneficiary the recipient of the profits that occur as a result of someone else's actions.

bequest similar to an inheritance, a transfer of personal property through a will.

betterment an upgrade to property.

bilateral contract a contract, such as a rent agreement, when both parties agree to comply with or not comply with certain terms.

bill of sale a legal paper that transfers ownership of property from one person (company) to another.

binder money paid to hold a property for set terms.

biweekly mortgage payments made on real estate every two weeks as opposed to once a month. In some cases, this reduces the time needed to pay off the loan.

blanket mortgage a mortgage owned by the same person on at least two properties.

blockbusting an illegal process that involves scaring residents of an area into selling their property at reduced prices so that an agent can take advantage of them.

bona fide legal adjective that describes faithful, trustworthy actions or people.

bond a type of insurance money that protects a professional against loss.

boot a sum of cash included in a buyer/seller agreement to even out exchange.

branch office a satellite or another office that is at a separate place from headquarters.

breach of contract breaking a binding agreement illegally.

bribery giving, receiving, or soliciting to influence an action, such as an illegal gratuity.

broker professional or entity that is qualified through classes and licensed to buy or sell property.

brokerage a firm that employs one or more real estate professionals; real estate company.

broker's price opinion (BPO) an estimate on the worth of real estate by a professional in the industry.

building code state and local legislation that regulates new edifices or structural changes or existing ones.

building line an invisible boundary line around the property. The building must stay within this boundary.

building restrictions state, local and neighborhood guidelines or constraints that guide how something is built or to determine property use.

bundle of rights privileges associated with property ownership, such as residency or use.

buy down payment by the buyer of added fees or points to the seller or lender for a lower interest rate.

buyer's broker a real estate professional who searches for a property and conducts negotiations in order to purchase the property.

bylaws procedural guidelines used to conduct business or meetings at an organization like a homeowners association.

>C

cancellation clause a section in a contract that permits parties to nullify the obligations of the contract.

canvassing surveying or soliciting an area to see if people are interested in selling their homes.

cap the maximum increase in interest for a mortgage with changing rates.

capital funds used to generate more money.

capital expenditure money spent to improve the value of real estate.

capital gains tax taxation on the proceeds from a property sale.

capitalization the total yearly potential earnings on a property, such as a rental.

capitalization rate a percentage that can be used to compare investment opportunities. This is determined by dividing the yearly capitalization by the cost of the property.

cash flow the final amount of income generated from a rental property after income and expenses.

caveat emptor Latin expression meaning "let the buyer beware." Serves as a warning to the buyer.

CC&R covenants, conditions and restrictions – the bylaws for a group of homeowners.

certificate of discharge an IRS document that enables the government to waive taxes on a property.

certificate of eligibility formal document from the Veterans Administration that proves the person qualifies for a VA loan.

certificate of reasonable value (CRV) the maximum value permitted for a VA mortgage.

certificate of sale permits the buyer to receive the title for the purchase of the property.

certificate of title an official decision on the ownership, status or availability of a piece of real estate through public documents.

chain of title the legal document that tells the history of a piece of real estate.

chattel any property someone owns except real estate.

chattel mortgage the use of personal property as security for debt repayment.

city an incorporated group of residences larger than a town or village.

clear title a document of ownership that is completely valid.

closing the final legal transfer of property ownership through the signing of official papers.

closing costs the monies associated with the sale of property, such as inspection fees.

closing date the actual date the property will transfer from the buyer to the seller.

closing statement a final summary of all costs involved in the sale of real estate.

cloud on the title a questionable title as to the availability for sale.

clustering a group of residential buildings used to maximize land use.

codicil an addendum to a will that explains additions or deletions to the document.

coinsurance clause a clause in an insurance policy that divides financial responsibility for a loss between at least two parties.

collateral something of value that promises the repayment of a loan.

collection efforts to acquire delinquent rent or mortgage payments.

color of title a title that is invalid although initially it seemed to be valid.

commercial property real estate set aside for business use.

commingling combining the funds of two parties in one account

commission the payment that a broker or real estate agent receives for the sale of a property, usually a percentage of the sale price.

commitment letter a document from the mortgage company that informs the borrower regarding loan approval and the terms of said approval.

common areas regions of a neighborhood or apartment complex that all residents share, such as a pool, playground or parking lot.

common law originating in England, law based in part on traditions and in part on the courts.

community property real estate and chattel shared by two parties, usually husband and wife.

comparable sales used to help determine current market value, the latest sales of similar properties in the area are comparable sales.

comparative market analysis (CMA) assessing the worth of real estate through a comparison of the value of similar pieces of real estate in the area. See comparable sales.

competent parties those who can legally enter into a contract.

condemnation taking over ownership of a property, usually by the government, and paying the owner for the real estate.

condominium similar to apartments, individual residences in a building or area with common areas shared jointly by all residents.

condominium conversion the transfer in ownership in a condominium from one owner to many for each residence.

conflict of interest occurs when there is a bias or self interest against a represented individual or organization.

conformity the belief that similar pieces of real estate will retain their worth.

consideration a legal enticement that attracts the buyer to sign the contract.

construction mortgage a two-part loan – first, to pay for construction costs and next to pay for the home. Usually the borrower pays interest-only payments until the home is finished when the mortgage is converted to a regular loan.

constructive eviction when a tenant moves out of a residence because of the poor quality of the residence without being liable for rent.

constructive notice public record and therefore common information to all.

contingency certain requirements that must be met to fulfill the contract

contract a legal arrangement between two legal parties that establishes certain conditions that will happen.

contract for deed a deferment of the payment of property for a specific time frame.

conventional loan financing to obtain a piece of property or real estate.

conversion option an agreement that the buyer can change an adjustable interest rate to a fixed rate. There is a cost-associated with this option.

convertible ARM an agreement that the buyer can change an adjustable interest rate to a fixed rate. There is a cost associated with this option.

conveyance the legal transfer of property from one party to another.

cooperative ownership in shares of a common residential building, similar to an apartment, which allows the owners to live there.

corporation a company acts as its own business with liability and management.

cost approach a way to estimate real estate value by starting with the worth of the property, subtracting costs and adding improvements.

counteroffer saying no to a real estate offer and then suggesting a different offer.

covenant specifications included in the deed requiring obligations or restrictions on real estate use.

covenant of seisin a legal verification that the owner has the right to the property.

credit available financial backing for real estate that needs to be repaid in the future.

credit history a list of creditors or lenders who have lent the individual money and a history of how the individual has fulfilled his financial obligations.

cul-de-sac a semi-private road with a circular type of dead-end, usually adds value in real estate.

curtesy a man's ownership of some or all of his spouse's property even if she will deny him such ownership.

curtilage the area in close proximity to a residence, including other buildings, but not including open lands away from the home.

>D

damages financial or other compensation to the hurt party for tangible or intangible losses.

datum a horizontal reference point used to make vertical measurements.

DBA "doing business as" – sometimes used as an "also known as" name for a company.

debt money or property that is owed to another and must be repaid.

debt service repayment over a specific time frame, usually of a mortgage, including interest and principal.

decedent a person who passed away, often used in discussions of their estate, will, inheritance or other financial matters.

dedication a gift of property for the benefit of all and the receipt of land by authorities.

deed the official, written proof that transfers and verifies property ownership.

deed-in-lieu used instead of a foreclosure, the property owner returns the property deed back to the lender to avoid a public record of foreclosure.

deed of trust a type of mortgage used in some jurisdictions.

deed restriction part of the deed that prevents the owner from certain land uses.

default failure to make a loan payment within a certain time frame, usually within 30 days of the due date.

defeasance clause the legal option that the lender has to repossess delinquent payments or the property from the borrower in case of a default.

deficiency judgment a legal document ordering the collection of the difference between what a borrower owes to the bank and the sale price of a home.

delinquency late payment on a loan.

density zoning regulations that prohibit more than a certain number of homes in an area.

depreciation a reduction in the value of an asset because of financial, physical or use.

descent the passing down of property to an heir if the deceased person has not left specific provisions.

devise a gift of real estate to an heir through a will.

devisee the person who receives a gift of property from a will.

devisor the person who gives a gift of property to another through a will.

directional growth the direction in which a city is expanding.

discount point money paid to the mortgage holder to reduce the interest payment. The more money that is paid, the lower the interest will fall.

discount rate the interest rate that a bank will pay to the Federal Reserve to borrow cash for short-term loans.

dispossess legal process of eviction.

divisible contract called a severable contract, has two or more components that act as independent contracts when breached.

dominant estate (tenement) property that benefits from the shared use of land on a neighboring property.

dower a woman's ownership of some or all of her spouse's property even if his will denies her such ownership.

down payment cash, as part of the cost of real estate, paid separately from the financing.

dual agency a real estate agent or broker who acts on behalf of two or more parties in a sale.

due-on-sale clause requires the loan to be repaid to the lender when the real estate is sold.

duress a person feels threatened into doing something, such as selling property.

>E

earnest money money to prove the buyer's serious intent of purchasing the home.

easement an agreement that one person has the privilege of use of another's land.

easement by necessity the need to walk on someone else's property by necessity.

easement by prescription accepted use of property by another person that is unnecessary. This becomes legal when it occurs over a certain number of years, such as a shortcut through a neighbor's yard.

easement in gross accepted use of property that remains with the individual and does not convey with the property. For example, when the home is sold to a different owner, the easements are not passed to the new owner.

economic life the length of time when real estate will continue to earn money.

effective age the age of the building based on the condition of the building.

emblements different types of farming crops considered part of property.

embezzlement the fraudulent conversion of property when the possession was given through a trust relationship.

eminent domain the purchase of private property by the government for public purposes.

encroachment part of real estate that crosses property boundaries onto another's property.

encumbrance assessments against a property, such as delinquent HOA fees, any mortgages or easements that impact the value.

equitable title the right someone has to a property when they commit to buy it although the deal is not yet finalized.

equity the worth of the property above the mortgage or other debts on the property.

equity of redemption the reclaiming of real estate by the mortgage holder because of foreclosure.

erosion slow wearing away of land by natural elements, such as flooding.

escalation clause passing on increased expenses to tenants, such as fuel or HOA fees.

escheat real estate goes to the state if a person dies without a will and without any heirs.

escrow money or something of value held in trust by a third party until the completion of a specific transaction.

escrow account monies collected from the buyer that the lender holds in reserve to pay property taxes and homeowner's insurance.

escrow analysis a yearly review that assesses the monies collected in escrow to ensure that the amount is correct. It may be increased or decreased at that time to reconcile the account.

escrow disbursements the use of the escrow account to pay taxes, insurances and expenses.

estate all of a person's property.

estate for years time frame during which a person accesses land or property.

estate tax the tax on the worth of the assets when a person dies. A certain portion of the estate is exempt.

estoppel written confirmation that the borrower signs stating that the mortgage amount is correct.

et al. Latin for "and others," used to refer to property ownership by several people, "Jane Doe, et. al."

et ux. Latin for "and wife."

et vir Latin for "and husband."

eviction the process by which a person is legally removed from a property.

evidence of title official paperwork that proves that someone owns the property.

examination of title history of the title although not as complete or detailed as a title search.

exchange similar business or investment properties that can be traded tax-free per IRS Code 1031.

exclusive agency listing a binding legal agreement that gives a single broker permission to sell real estate for a certain time frame.

exclusive right to sell a binding legal agreement that gives the real estate agent the right to collect the commission if anyone else sells the property during the specified time frame.

exculpatory clause permits the borrower to give back the real estate to the lien holder without personal responsibility to pay the mortgage.

execution when a creditor wants to enforce the payment of the debt, he will require the debtor to turn over the property.

executor/executrix the person established by the deceased to perform estate duties. Executrix is a female who performs these duties.

executory contract a legal agreement that is awaiting action by at least one party for completion.

executed contract a completed contract.

express contract details all aspects of the contract, such as offer, acceptance, and consideration.

extension agreement a mutual decision to lengthen the time frame for performance of a contract.

external obsolescence a reduction in the worth of a specific home improvement because of something separate from the real estate that decreases the worth of the home.

>F

fair housing law a national statute that prohibits discrimination in any housing dealings because of race, color, sex, religion, family status, handicap (disability) or national origin.

fair market value what the property will sell for according to both buyer and seller.

Federal Housing Administration (FHA) a government agency that guarantees loans to make housing easier to obtain.

Federal National Mortgage Association (Fannie Mae) a federal organization that helps keep the home loan market solvent by purchasing notes from bankers.

Federal Reserve System the government banking system that oversees banks, offers services and sets national economic policy.

fee simple full and complete ownership of real estate.

FHA-insured loan a mortgage that is backed by the government through the FHA. VA loans are also backed by the government.

fiduciary relationship a person who acts on another's behalf in business or general matters.

finder's fee money that the realtor pays to a third party who finds a buyer, usually illegal.

first mortgage the first loan taken out on a home, usually in chronological order, but not always.

fixed-rate loan a loan where the interest rate remains the same throughout the loan term.

fixture personal property affixed to the building that conveys with the building when it is sold.

foreclosure the process by which a buyer loses the property because of failure to pay the debt, which results in the public sale of the real estate in order to pay as much of the debt as possible.

forfeiture seizure of property because of criminal actions or failure to fulfill a contract.

franchise when a business owner pays to use a company name in return for company backing, such as member brokerages.

fraud deceptive actions intended to mislead another person and harm them

freehold estate continued ownership or stake in a property as compared to a temporary stake or a lease.

front foot the measurement at the front of the home nearest the street; used to compare home value, especially on the same street.

functional obsolescence the decrease in worth of the real estate except that caused by wear and tear.

future interest a right to real estate that will occur in the future.

>G

general agent someone who can do any job duties related to the business on behalf of the principal. A real estate agent acts as a special agent.

general lien a mortgage that covers more than one property owned by the same person.

general warranty deed a guarantee that the title is free and clear of other claims against it for the protection of the buyer.

government-backed mortgage a loan that is backed by the federal government as contrasted with a conventional loan.

Government National Mortgage Association (Ginnie Mae) a federal agency that supplies funding for government loans.

government survey system a process of dividing land into rectangular sections in order to set area boundaries.

graduated lease a rental agreement that permits periodic adjustments in rental price increases.

grant the transfer of real estate to another party through a deed.

grant deed the legal document used to transfer real estate to another.

grantee the person who receives the real estate; buyer.

grantor the person who sells the real estate.

gross income all financial gains received for real estate before any losses or expenses on the property.

gross income multiplier a way to assess the profitability of property arrived at by dividing the total price paid, or the value of the property by the annual gross income.

gross lease a rental agreement wherein the landlord pays all costs associated with the property, including HOA fees, repairs, taxes, and more.

ground lease a lease of land only, not of buildings.

guaranteed sale plan a contract between the seller and the real estate agent/broker. The broker promises to buy the property for predetermined terms if the property does not sell by a certain date.

guardian a person whom the court deems legally responsible for someone who is incapable of managing his affairs.

>H

habendum clause "to have and to hold" that specifies any restrictions on property; fee simple absolute.

hamlet a small, populated area; municipality.

heir someone who receives property, often through a will after a death.

hereditament anything either tangible or intangible that can be given through a will.

highest and best use the most productive use of real estate that will provide the greatest financial return over a specified period of time.

holdover tenancy a renter who stays on the property when the lease ends.

holographic will a handwritten will signed by the person who makes the will; does not need a notary or witness.

home equity conversion mortgage (HECM) reverse mortgage or when a lender makes payments, usually monthly, to a homeowner.

home equity line of credit a loan available to homeowners based on the equity in the home.

home inspection a professional assessment of the real estate that closely examines the property.

homeowners association (HOA) a corporation or private party formed by a real estate developer and designed to market, manage or sell homes in a subdivision area.

homeowner's insurance an insurance policy that covers the property and contents against all types of natural and other damages, includes liability.

homeowner's warranty insurance coverage that protects the buyer against any defects in the residence.

homestead permitted by some states, protects a residence against lawsuits or judgments up to certain limits.

Housing Urban and Development Department (HUD) federal agency that regulates some aspects of the housing industry.

hypothecate a promise of something as pledge for a loan without physically relinquishing that item. Most homeowners live in their primary residence through this method unless they own the residence free and clear.

>I

implied contract an informal contract, not in writing, yet enforceable by the courts.

improvement work done on land or property that increases worth, additions or upgrades that are more consequential than repairs.

income capitalization approach a specific formula used to assess the income-producing worth of a property.

income property real estate that earns money for the owner.

incorporeal right intangible rights associated with real estate, such as easements and future income.

indemnify to insure against loss.

independent contractor the employment status of most real estate agents; those who work independently and do not have an employer/employee relationship.

index an assessment of the current financial atmosphere by the government; used to adjust prices.

industrial property real estate used for nonresidential but business purposes, such as a warehouse or manufacturing property.

inflation an increase in overall costs and expenses that results in a decrease in what money will buy.

initial interest rate the first or starting rate for an adjustable mortgage.

installment a scheduled payment toward the reduction of debt, such as a mortgage.

installment contract a binding, legal, written agreement that sets a schedule for the loan payments.

installment loan a loan that is repaid in periodic payments at a set schedule; sometimes secured by personal property.

installment sale payments made to a seller over a longer period of time in order to defer taxes.

insurance money paid to an indemnity holder to reduce the expenses associated with the specific emergencies being insured, such as flooding or earthquakes.

insurance binder temporary proof of insurance until the permanent paperwork is completed.

insured mortgage financial backing for a loan that protects the lender against default, sometimes called PMI.

interest a legal right to real estate or other property; the amount a lender charges a borrower for the loan above the principal, usually specified as a percentage.

interest accrual rate how often the interest accrues, such as daily, weekly or monthly, until it is paid to the lender.

interest rate the amount a lender charges a borrower for the loan above the principal, usually specified as a percentage.

interest rate buy down plan using money from a still uncompleted home sale to reduce the interest rate and the monthly costs to the buyer.

interest rate ceiling the maximum percentage rate cap on an adjustable rate mortgage.

interest rate floor the lowest percentage rate minimum on an adjustable rate mortgage.

interim financing a transitional loan to bridge the time frame until the buyer can obtain permanent financing, for example a construction loan.

intestate without a legal will or without any will at all.

invalid not legally enforceable, such as a will or a contract.

investment property real estate purchased for the purpose of generating income.

>J

joint tenancy more than one individual who owns property in common, usually related individuals.

joint venture more than one entity who works toward the same professional goal, usually a temporary arrangement for a specific purpose.

judgment the court order that sets the amount one person or entity owes another in the event of a default, such as a loan or an eviction.

judgment lien a lender's right to claim the property of the borrower because of a judgment.

judicial foreclosure court order to force the sale of real estate to pay off debt. The satisfaction of debts will stop foreclosure.

jumbo loan a property loan above the normal limits.

junior mortgage a loan that will only be satisfied after the first mortgage.

>L

laches the delay of the time during which a legal claim can be enforced.

land solid real estate, separate from water or air.

land cover the physical cover on the earth.

landlocked property that is not accessible to public roads except through a neighboring property.

land use the activities of people on the land.

land use analysis studies land use to find efficient patterns.

lease a legal contract that lasts for a specific period during which the owner allows the renter to possess the property.

leased fee a restriction on property because of a rental/lease agreement.

lease option the renter can decide to buy the property under certain conditions.

leasehold property subject to a long-term rental agreement.

legal description authoritative confirmation of a property through written, technical means.

lessee tenant of real estate property.

lessor landlord of real estate property.

leverage the mortgage used to purchase a home or business.

levy a legal order of payment of any money due.

license legal permission, such as the temporary use of property.

lien financial assessment against real estate that must be paid when the land is sold.

life estate a lifelong interest in a specific real estate that ends when the owner dies.

life tenant someone who can stay on the real estate property until their death.

liquidity the availability of cash when using assets, such as property or real estate.

lis pendens Latin for "suit pending." Notice of possible restrictions on title when a lawsuit is filed.

listing agreement a contract between a real estate agent and client that pays commission to the agent no matter how the buyer finds the property.

listing broker the real estate agent who lists the property.

littoral rights the shore land next to an ocean or very large water body that the property owner has rights to.

loan borrowing money from another entity.

loan officer a representative for the lender or for the borrower to the lender who may also look for loans.

lock-in the borrower pays a fee to guarantee a certain interest rate for a specific time period, especially if the borrower thinks the interest rates will rise.

lock-in period the time frame of the lock-in, such as 90 days.

lot and block description a legal process of finding real estate based on its lot and block identification within the housing area.

>M

management agreement a legal agreement between an owner and a property manager for a percentage of the rental generated.

margin a flat percentage to adjust interest rates up or down according to the index used in adjustable rate mortgages.

market data approach a comparison of recent property sales to assess real estate worth.

market value in real estate, price range between the maximum purchase price and minimum purchase price.

marketable title a free-and-clear title.

mechanic's lien a hold on the construction and on the real estate that guarantees payment for the work done on the property.

metes and bounds specific description of the land that identifies all boundaries of the real estate.

mill one-tenth of a penny; used for taxation.

minor a person who is not of legal age to make a binding decision.

misrepresentation a misleading verbalization even if unintended.

modification a legal alteration to a contract.

money judgment a court order that orders a financial payment.

month-to-month tenancy a rental agreement that can be extended or cancelled each month.

monument a landmark or immovable object used to decide the land locations.

mortgage a loan on property that uses the property itself as security for the repayment of the property.

mortgage banker a bank that finances loans for others, which are then sometimes purchased by federal agencies.

mortgage broker an agency that researches and finds loans for others but does not finance them.

mortgage lien the financing on a piece of real estate that obligates the buyer to the holder.

mortgagee the person/agency who lends money in a real estate transaction.

mortgagor the person/agency who borrows money in a real estate transaction.

multi-dwelling units a building, such as an apartment complex, that has separate living units but only one property loan.

multiple-listing system (MLS, also service) a group of real estate agents that lists all the available properties for sale, which gives a buyer a wide range of choices.

mutual rescission an agreement to void a contract by all involved parties.

>N

negative amortization a deferment of interest payments on a loan, which is added on to the principal and results in an eventual increase in the payments over time and a loss of value on the home.

net income when all bills have been paid, the earnings that remain.

net lease the renter, as opposed to the landlord, pays costs, such as HOA fees, repairs and upkeep.

net listing any funds above the original price of the property that are paid to the real estate agent, illegal in some places.

net worth the positive, monetary difference between the value of assets and liabilities.

no cash-out refinance sometimes called a "rate and term refinance," the borrower receives no cash, but the money is used to recalculate the loan and related costs.

non-conforming use a code violation related to property use that is permitted because it was "grandfathered in." In other words, the property owner began the questionable property use before the zoning ordinance took effect.

non-liquid asset something of worth that is difficult to convert to cash.

notarize to witness the veracity of a signature.

notary public a person with the legal and official authority to witness the veracity of a signature.

note the written loan that admits debt and promises repayment.

note rate the interest rate on a loan or mortgage.

notice of default official notification that the borrower has defaulted and that the lender can take additional legal remedies.

novation the substitution of one party for another party in a contract.

>O

obligee a person requesting a certain duty in their favor.

obligor a person required to perform a certain duty, often under bond.

obsolescence a decrease in worth because of outdated design or construction, such as a home without a dishwasher or cable hook-up.

offer a suggestion or expression of desire to buy or sell real estate.

offer and acceptance the suggestion or expression of desire to buy or sell real estate and the acceptance of the offer by the other party.

open-end mortgage a loan with smaller amount than the maximum funds that a borrower can access from the lender.

open listing more than one real estate agent can list the property; the first to close the sale is the one who receives payment.

opinion of title legal authentication that the title is clear.

option an agreement that allows a buyer to purchase a property at a specific price if done so within a specific time period.

optionee the person who has available choices.

optionor the person who gives or sells the available choices.

ordinance a statute or legislation related to property use.

original principal balance the loan amount before the first payment is made.

origination fee fees assessed to the borrower that cover loan expenses related to the title, appraisal and credit checks.

owner financing the seller provides the buyer with the loan; the buyer does not go through a bank.

ownership possession of property.

>P

package mortgage a combination loan that covers both the residence and the land.

parcel a section of real estate under the person who owns it.

participation mortgage a loan that permits the holder to receive a portion of the profits from the property.

partition equal division of property between all owners.

partnership business relationship between two or more parties subject to debt and tax laws.

party wall divides two properties with ownership rights for both users.

payee the seller who receives money or something of value.

payor the buyer who gives the payee money or something of value.

percentage lease a rental payment determined by sales volume of the renter with a minimum rental amount.

periodic estate a rental agreement that goes for a specific time frame, such as month-to-month.

personal property (hereditaments) anything either tangible or intangible given through a will.

physical deterioration decrease in property worth because of normal wear, failure to repair, or things breaking.

PITI principal, interest, taxes and insurance payment; usually the total of all payments due on the property.

planned unit development (PUD) zoning permission to design a subdivision with flexibility and creativity.

plat description of a section of land that provides detailed information about the area.

plat book public information with the description of a section of land that provides detailed information about the area.

plat number the number associated with each lot in a plat.

plottage combining small sections of real estate into a larger parcel.

PMI private mortgage insurance; used to cover the default of the loan.

point one percent of the loan amount; monies paid to entice a lender to lend money to the borrower, sometimes used in exchange for a reduction in the interest rate on the loan.

point of beginning the same starting and ending point on a land survey as the survey borders and encloses the property.

police power the government's ability to address the overall well being of the community.

power of attorney the legal right for one person to perform duties for another either some or all of the time.

preapproval qualifying a buyer prior to purchase of the home.

prepayment paying costs or monies due early, sometimes as escrow funds.

prepayment penalty the expenses associated with early payoff of a loan.

prequalification preapproval, sometimes in writing, before the buyer can purchase the home.

prescription receiving the right to a property through common use, such as a squatter, or adverse possession.

primary mortgage market the original buyer of a loan, such as a bank or savings and loan, which may then be sold on the secondary mortgage market for a profit.

prime rate the lowest available interest rate a lending institution charges on short-term loans to businesses.

principal the face value of a loan or mortgage, separate from the interest, taxes and insurance.

principal meridian an imaginary north/south line used as a reference point in surveying to describe land.

probate to confirm the authenticity of a will.

procuring cause a method of deciding if the real estate agent earned a commission, legal expression that means the goal was realized through the actions.

promissory note a written statement of a promise to pay.

property management oversight of different aspects of property, such as collecting payments, upkeep, leasing units, cleaning units.

property tax real estate tax based on worth that is collected by the government.

prorate to equally divide a financial assessment between a buyer and a seller, for example as HOA fees or property taxes.

pur autre vie "For the life of another," use of property that one individual gives another, as long as a third person is alive.

purchase agreement also called contract of sale or agreement of sale; a written contract between a buyer and seller.

purchase money mortgage a mortgage loan that the purchaser owes to the seller as partial payment for property.

>Q

qualifying ratios the ratio of the buyer's debt when compared to the buyer's income, which must be below a certain percentage for a lending institution to offer the loan.

quitclaim deed a release of rights in a property without confirming the validity or the rights of the person who keeps the deed.

range a six-mile-wide area of land. Using the rectangular survey system, it is labeled east or west.

ready, willing, and able a buyer who is ready to buy and follows through with the requirements needed to close the sale.

real estate land, the air above it, the ground under it and any buildings on it.

real estate agent a person who acts on the behalf of another to make a transaction with a third party.

real estate board a group of professional agents who belong to the National Association of Realtors.

real estate broker a person who acts on behalf of another to make a transaction with a third party.

Real Estate Settlement Procedures Act (RESPA) a law that informs buyers of their rights by requiring the lender to give updated information to the borrower throughout the home-buying process.

real property real estate, physical land and structures on the land.

realtor a professional real estate agent.

recording the official documentation related to a change in property title, such as by a sale or transfer.

rectangular survey system a survey method of dividing land into squares and grids.

redemption period a time frame when an owner can buy back real estate that was foreclosed.

redlining illegal action of refusing to lend money to an individual in a lower socio-economic area without considering the circumstances of the individual.

refinance transaction obtaining a new loan on real estate and paying off an earlier loan using the same real estate as collateral.

Regulation Z federal requirement that a lender must disclose all terms of a loan, including the APR.

release clause a section in a contract that allows the buyer to pay off part of the loan, which then frees a piece of the real estate from being security for the loan.

remainder estate the real estate that passes to another individual when the first individual's rights in the real estate end.

remainderman the individual to whom real estate goes when a life tenant dies.

remaining balance the amount still left to pay on a loan.

remaining term the length of time still left to pay on a loan.

rent payment for temporary use of property; lease.

replacement cost the amount of money needed to replicate an edifice so that it can fulfill previous functions.

reproduction cost the amount of money needed for an exact replica of an edifice.

rescission the negating of a contract so that it is no longer in effect.

restriction (restrictive covenant) prevents the real estate from being used in certain manners, either in the deed or through local laws.

reversion the landlord's right to take possession of rental property when the rental agreement ends.

reversionary interest the interest the remainderman has in the ownership of the real estate as it passes to them when a life tenant dies.

reverse annuity mortgage a property loan used for a person with high equity when the lender makes yearly payments to the homeowner.

revision alteration or change (e.g. of a contract).

right of egress (or ingress) the right to leave real estate; the right to go to real estate.

right of first refusal the option an individual or entity has to fulfill a legal agreement before another person or entity meets those obligations.

right of redemption the owner's privilege to take possession of real estate when the financial obligations of the loan have been met even during the process of foreclosure.

right of survivorship the remaining survivor's right to take over the interest of a deceased owner.

riparian rights water rights in close proximity to a person's real estate

safety clause an extender clause or protection clause that gives the broker a commission if a buyer who sees the home returns later to close the sale.

sale-leaseback the sale of real estate to a new owner who then rents the real estate back to the original owner.

sales contract a legal agreement between a buyer and seller to finalize a sale.

salesperson a professional and licensed real estate agent or broker.

salvage value used to determine depreciation; the worth of a property or asset when its service is over.

satisfaction a document that verifies and confirms the mortgage payoff.

second mortgage a mortgage obtained after the first mortgage used for a down payment, refinancing or cash.

section a unit of measurement in the government rectangular system, one-square mile.

secured loan a loan that uses collateral in the case of default.

security the property used as collateral in case of default when money is borrowed.

seisin the owner who holds the title to the property free and clear.

selling broker the real estate agent who finds a buyer for the property.

separate property property that belongs to only one spouse as opposed to both spouses.

servient tenement property that gives shared use of land to a neighboring property for their good.

setback a boundary away from the edge of the property that must remain free of buildings.

settlement statement (HUD-1) a full accounting of all the monetary transactions that occur in a property sale.

severalty independent interest in real estate by a person.

special assessment a financial levy against real estate to pay for something of benefit to that real estate.

special warranty deed a deed that pertains only to the title under the person issuing it, not to any title issues from previous title holders.

specific lien a mortgage or lien against only a specified part of the real estate.

specific performance mandate by the court that the party in a contract fulfill their duties.

standard payment calculation a process of calculating monthly equal payments needed to pay the balance owed on a mortgage at the present interest rate.

statute of frauds legal necessity for real estate contracts to be written in order to be enforceable.

statute of limitations a time period after which someone cannot file a lawsuit.

statutory lien a legal obligation on the property, such as taxes.

steering illegal action when only certain racial or cultural groups are shown a property.

straight-line depreciation the total depreciation divided by the number of years of depreciation.

subdivision a division of land into lots upon which homes are built.

sublet to rent from another renter.

subordinate a lesser priority, as in a subordinate mortgage that would be paid off only if the first mortgage was satisfied in a foreclosure.

substitution replacing the market worth of one piece of real estate for another piece of real estate, usually viewed as indifferent by buyers.

subrogation the legal substitution of one individual for another individual, with all rights passing onto the new party.

suit for possession eviction lawsuit after a break of contract by a renter.

suit for specific performance a lawsuit filed by the buyer for breach of contract in property sale. The court can either require the seller to pay damages and expenses or complete the sale.

survey the boundaries of a parcel of real estate; a map of the property surveyed.

syndicate a group of people or entities who join resources to invest in real estate.

>T

tax deed a legal document that places a claim on real estate because of owed taxes.

tax lien a hold placed on real estate because of owed taxes prior to filing the tax deed.

tax rate the rate at which an individual property is taxed; calculated by dividing all funds needed by all properties within the locale.

tax sale the sale of real estate because taxes have not been paid.

tenancy at sufferance a renter who can no longer legally remain on the property because the lease has ended.

tenancy at will an agreement the owner provides to the renter that ends if and when the landlord decides to end it. The renter can also terminate the lease.

tenancy by the entirety equal rights to property shared between spouses, the real estate passes to the surviving spouse upon death of a spouse.

tenancy in common equal rights to property shared between individuals without surviving rights but determined through a will upon one party's death.

tenant renter who pays the landlord a fee for property use.

tenement a fixture that remains as part of the land.

testate a person who dies with a legal will in place.

"time is of the essence" following a contract according to time specifications to prevent delays in fulfilling the contract.

time sharing a piece of real estate owned by more than one person; each person has the right to a specific time at the property.

title legal proof and verification of property ownership.

title insurance insurance that covers the owner from problems with the title.

title search scrutiny of legal records to review the rights to and encumbrances against real estate.

Torrens system a shortcut type of title registration available in some jurisdictions without going through the lengthy process of a title search.

township a section of land in the government rectangular survey system; six square miles.

trade fixtures fixtures, such as furniture and appliances, used in a specific business; may convey with the property upon the expiration of the lease.

transfer tax an assessment levied when a title passes from one person or entity to another.

trust a holding that transfers the real estate to the trustee for the beneficiary.

trustee the person who keeps the real estate for the beneficiary.

Truth-in-Lending Law federal requirement that a lender must disclose all terms of a loan, including the APR.

>U

underwriting similar to insuring; validating the policy.

undivided interest shared rights and ownership of property among all owners.

unilateral contract one party has a duty to fulfill a certain responsibility in the contract but the other party does not.

unsecured loan a loan that uses no collateral but may be based on the borrower's credit worthiness.

useful life the period of time during which improvements will yield income.

usury charging a higher than maximum interest rate; illegal.

>V

VA-guaranteed loan a mortgage backed by the government agency, the Veterans Administration, which promises repayment to the lender for the main residence.

valid contract a legally binding contract that will hold up in a court of law.

valuation estimate of the price of real estate.

variance a deviation from zoning laws that permits the owner to violate zoning code.

vendee buyer of personal property.

vendor seller of personal property.

village a small grouping of residential properties and other buildings.

void contract a written agreement that cannot be enforced even when signed.

voidable contract a written agreement that becomes unenforceable after it is signed.

>W

waiver the abdication of certain rights.

warranty deed a legal right of protection against any type of claim.

waste specified abuse of mortgage or rental property that causes damages.

will legal document that transfers ownership of property to another upon the death of the person who writes the will.

wraparound mortgage a property loan that combines a first mortgage with a second mortgage at a higher loan amount and higher payment.

writ of execution an order that permits the court to sell the person's real estate, such as after a foreclosure.

>Z

zone a section regulated by local rules and conditions, such as a business zone that is prohibited from residential housing.

zoning ordinance a regulation that specifies the type of property use permitted in the area.

Real Estate Sales Exam I

1. A couple executes a sales contract on their home after several counteroffers with the buyer. In this case, the seller is:

a) the mortgagee

b) the grantor

c) the grantee

d) the mortgagor

2. The Cambridge family bought a house with a lot size of a quarter of an acre. This is equivalent to:

a) 10,890 square feet

b) 43,560 square feet

c) 11,000 square feet

d) 5,250 square feet

43,560 = 1 acre

40,560
x .25

sq ft

3. A primary residence is sold for $527,000 by a couple in the 28% tax bracket. The home was originally purchased by them eight years ago for $313,000 where the family lived for the entire eight years. How much will be paid in capital gain tax?

a) $59,920

b) $32,100

c) $214,000

d) none of the above

They lived in Home for more then 2 yrs

4. An owner-occupied four-unit dwelling worth $525,000 generates $4,500 in monthly income from three units and $150 a month from the onsite laundry. If the current owner typically yields roughly 9% annually on his investment, what is the monthly effective gross amount?

a) $4,350

b) $6,000

c) $4,905

d) $4,650

5. A brother is moving out of the country and decides to sell his home to his sister for $275,000, making this the latest sale in that area. The sister decides to pay cash, as she says

she will later get a home equity loan for $200,000. Recent sales comps of very similar homes had values of $325,000. Based on the information provided, what is best estimate of the market value of the subject property?

a) $325,000

Because they are related.

b) $200,000

c) $275,000

d) not enough information provided

6. A breach of contract is when:

a) only one person signs the contract

b) both parties choose to end the contract

c) both parties complete their duties stated in the contract

d) one party in a contract fails to complete their duties stated in the contract

7. A seller provides written permission allowing his listing broker (who has a fiduciary obligation to the seller) to work with the buyer. This relationship is known as:

a) dual agency

b) sub agency

c) special agency

d) implied agency

8. A homeowner purchased a home for $300,000 on a 30-year FHA loan with an interest rate of 4.25%. If he wants to do cash-out conventional refinance and eliminate the MIP, what is the largest of these amounts that the new loan balance can be based on a future home value of $350,000?

a) $276,500

b) $310,000

c) $300,000

d) $240,000

9. Which of these can be a valid contract?

A: a verbal agreement

B: a 10-month lease

a) both A and B

b) B only

c) neither A nor B

d) A only

10. A brother is moving out of the country and decides to sell his home to his sister for $275,000, making this home the latest sale in that area. This sister puts 20% down and finances $220,000. Recent sales comps of similar homes had values of $485,000. Based on the information provided, what is the market value?

a) $485,000

b) $220,000

c) $225,000

d) not enough information provided

not a considered comp

11. Which best describes an example of emblements? *annually cropped*

a) cherry tree, apple tree, and tomato plants

b) cherry tree, apple tree, and peach tree

c) tomato, lettuce, and onion crops

d) none of these

12. Nine states recognize this system of property ownership where the husband and wife have equal interest in property acquired during marriage. This is_____.

a) common law

b) community property

c) commingling

d) common title

13. A dad who owns his house free and clear decides to take out a HELOC and let his son make the payments. He also signs a quitclaim deed to transfer the home into his son's name. What clause might the lender enforce?

a) co-insurance clause

b) acceleration clause

c) due-on-sale clause

d) cancellation clause

14. A couple in Virginia requests the name of an excellent home inspector from their agent. All are things the realtor should do EXCEPT which of the following?

a) provide them with a brochure

b) tell them that it is a conflict for her to recommend an inspector

c) give them a list of at least five home inspectors

d) direct them to the state home inspection website

15. The Federal Home Loan Mortgage Corporation primarily purchases which loan types?

a) FHA

b) owner-financed notes

c) VA

d) conventional

16. Sally works for ABC Bank. Her job duties are to gather documents, review the application for accuracy, package the loan, and take each file from pre-approval to closing. What is most likely her job title?

a) underwriter

b) processor

c) loan officer

d) appraiser

17. Which of the following does not lend money directly to borrowers?

a) insurance company

b) mortgage broker

c) cooperative bank

d) private lender

18. Jay decides that he's ready to move out of his parents' home and purchase his own home. He has a roommate who will be moving in so he would like at least a three-bedroom house. What should his first step be?

a) get prequalified by submitting a mortgage application

b) purchase new furniture

c) pick out a house

d) purchase a new car to go with the new house

19. Mike and Kathy have $30,000 or 10% down to purchase their first home. Their loan officer prequalifies them for several different loan types. They decide to go with the following scenario: purchase price $300,000, with a loan amount of $300,000 and a $6,450 funding fee. What type of loan did they choose?

a) conventional

b) FHA

c) VA

d) negative amortization

20. A lender offers you a very low interest of 2.75% in exchange for part of your equity. What type of mortgage is this?

a) balloon

b) shared equity

c) wraparound mortgage

d) equity loan

21. Sellers Keith and Rita execute a standard purchase and sale agreement on November first. The contract also states that by November 15th their agent should receive a mortgage commitment letter. November 14th, the buyer's agent sends over a letter that the buyer has been unable to secure financing. The buyer should expect:

a) their earnest money deposit back

b) to withdraw from the transaction

c) both a and b

d) neither a nor b

22. House and Home Realty Brokerage leased a two-family residence for $1,500 a month for each unit. Tenant 1 wrote a check to cover the first month's rent and deposit and Tenant 2 paid by money order. Which is the best representation of what the brokerage must do?

a) make and keep a copy of the payments collected from each tenant

b) nothing as long as the broker received the money that is sufficient

c) only copy the money order because a check is a legal record

d) tell the tenant to pay the owner directly

23. Kimberly finds the home of her dreams, a cozy bungalow built in 1932. Her agent suspects that the home may have lead-based paint. Kimberly has how many days to test for lead-based paint?

a) 5

b) 3

c) 7

d) 10

24. The Governor appoints nine members to the Real Estate Board. How many members are not licensed agents?

a) 5

b) none; all are licensed

c) 1

d) 2

25. An appraisal is done on a unique property that sits on 42.5 acres. The approach the appraiser will more than likely use is _____.

a) assumption

b) cost

c) income

d) market data

26. Jill secures a 15-year fixed conventional home loan. This loan was more than likely purchased by which investor?

a) FNMA

b) insurance company

c) an orb

d) GNMA

27. A homeowner has an existing mortgage balance of $120,000 with a mortgage payment of $1,375. He puts an ad in the newspaper to sell his home, owner financing where he will offer the buyer a new note based on a sales price of $258,000 at 5%. The buyer decides to use this financing to purchase the home. Based on the information given, what type of mortgage is this?

a) wraparound mortgage

b) junior mortgage

c) package mortgage

d) none of these

28. When determining whether a buyer is a good credit risk, the lender needs to evaluate:

a) borrower's credit, the borrower's ability to pay, and homeowner's age

b) ability to pay, property, borrower's 401(k)

c) borrower's credit, future expected value of the property, job stability

d) property, ability to pay, credit

29. When a buyer chooses to pay discount points, her goal is to receive_____.

a) cash back at closing

b) a lower interest rate

c) principal reduction

d) none of these

30. Kevin's sister decides she wants to purchase a home and needs to get prequalified. Kevin's sister's best friend James is a loan officer at the bank and tells him once the loan closes he will give him a referral fee. Which statement is true?

a) As long as James gives Kim the HUD information booklet within three days, he can pay a referral fee.

b) James is protected under RESPA.

c) James must disclose the referral amount on the GFE.

d) Fees and kickbacks to individuals who do not provide a loan is prohibited.

31. Members of the Virginia Real Estate Board serve a term of _____ years.

a) 5

b) 4   *Same as President*

c) 7

d) 10

32. The purpose of which of the following laws is to prohibit discrimination on the basis of race (only) in the sale of real property?

a) Gramm-Leach-Bliley Act (GLBA)

b) Virginia Consumer Protection Law

c) Federal Civil Rights Act of 1866

d) Federal Fair Housing Act of 1868

33. Another name for a HUD-1 is _____,

a) Good Faith Estimate

b) Uniform Settlement Statement

c) Truth in Lending document

d) Housing Uniform document

34. A homeowner attempts a refinance on his home only to find out that the home has two liens from the previous owner that were never paid off. Who should he contact?

a) the title insurance company

b) the escrow office

c) the loan officer

d) a real estate attorney

35. All listing types below allow the seller the right to sell their property on their own without paying a commission,
EXCEPT_____.

a) an exclusive agency

b) open

c) exclusive right to sell

d) none of the above

36. Kurt receives a letter that an expressway is being built where his property sits. The state offers to purchase his home. What right is the state exercising?

a) escheatment

b) foreclosure

c) adverse possession

d) eminent domain

37.   A family leases a home with a pool. The contract states that the owner will pay property taxes and insurance, but the tenant must pay the pool and yard expenses. This is known as a _____lease.

a) percentage

b) gross

c) net

d) month-to-month

38. Mr. Green has purchased new energy efficient windows, put weather stripping around the doors and replaced his old wall heater with a new central air and heat system. Mr. Green has _____ his home.

a) weatherized

b) energized

c) overhauled

d) redlined

39. Tenant James is renting a one-bedroom apartment and his rent will be $923 per month. If the cost to replace the lock and key is $150 and the security deposit is the same as the rent, what is the maximum amount of funds James may be asked to give to the owner?

a) $923

b) $2,919

c) $1,073

d) $1,996

40. The total commission for the sale of a $449,000 property is 6%. The listing states that they will offer 3.5% to a co-broker who brings a buyer which ends in a successfully closed transaction. How much will the listing broker net after his sales agent, who is on a 45/55 (listing broker gets 55%) split, is paid?

a) $26,940

b) $15,715

c) $6,174

d) $11,225

41. Several first-time home buyers purchasing homes in a community redevelopment area noticed that they were not offered a fixed-rate loan by the developer's lender. They were only offered adjustable rate mortgages. This is most likely an example of _____.

a) economic adjustments

b) redlining

c) conforming

d) steering

42. Susie has been a licensed sales agent for over a year and would like to pursue her broker's license. What must she do?

a) pass the test

b) provide proof that she has been an active salesperson for at least 36 of the last 48 months

c) be at least 18-years-old

d) all of the above

43. All are false except:

a) real estate licenses are valid for two years

b) an inactive sales agent cannot collect referral fees

c) the fee for renewing a salesperson's license is $40.50

d) a salesperson must take 300 hours of continuing education in order to remain in active status

44. FHA insured loans protect the:

a) lender

b) realtor

c) seller

d) buyer

45. The Virginia Condominium Act relates to which residence type?

a) three-family home

b) SFR

c) condo

d) mixed use property

46. A tenant signs a one-year lease that allows him to occupy the property during this time. This is an example of _____.

a) fee simple

b) freehold estate

c) time share

d) non-freehold estate

47. What is the form used in Virginia when the landlord wants the tenant to either comply with the terms of the lease or leave the premises?

a) Notice to Vacate

b) Notice to Quit

c) Notice of Compliance

d) Notice of Eviction

48. When someone who is upside down with his mortgage gets permission to sell his house for less than he owes, this process is known as:

a) short sale

b) foreclosure

c) deed restructure

d) deed-in-lieu of foreclosure

49. "OLD CAR" stands for:

a) obligation, litigation, disclosure, care, access, real estate

b) obedience, loyalty, dedication, confidentiality, accountability, realtor

c) obligation, license, disclosure, confidentiality, accountability, reasonable care

d) obedience, loyalty, disclosure, confidentiality, accountability, reasonable care

50. A couple's agent takes them to see a for-sale-by-owner listing. The couple decides they really like the house and make an offer. The seller, impressed by the agent's professionalism, asks if she can represent him also. This type of agency is_____.

a) a facilitator

b) prohibited in Virginia

c) a dual agency

d) a buyer's agent

51. A broker's license can be revoked if he:

a) fails to return deposit funds to client when requested

b) commingles business and personal funds

c) fails to pay the agent his commission split

d) any of the above

52. A person dies leaving no will and no heirs. The decedent's property would transfer by:

a) adverse possession

b) state

c) escheat

d) laws of descent

53. Describe the ownership of a property if four cousins, Keenan, Kelly, Shon, and Marcia are joint tenants and Marcia sells her interest to cousin Michael. The new deed will read:

a) tenants in common with Keenan, Kelly and Shon

b) tenants at will

c) joints tenant Keenan, Kelly and Shon

d) Marcia is not allowed to sell her interest

54. A transaction where the seller agrees to finance the loan of the buyer is called:

a) hard money loan

b) blanket mortgage

c) conventional loan

d) purchase money mortgage

55. A 2,980-square-foot home sells for $328,000. If it sits on an acre lot, what is the price per square foot the home sold for?

a) $94

b) $110

c) $116

d) $154

56. A lot recently sold for $198,000. It is 378' x 296.' What was the cost per acre?

a) $67,074

b) $70,774

c) $77,774

d) $77,042

57. If Michelle sells her home, but then remains in the property by becoming a tenant of the new landlord, this is known as:

a) testate

b) wraparound mortgage

c) leaseback

d) freehold

58. A homeowner puts a $104,250 down payment on a $417,000 home. What percentage is the down payment?

a) 25%

b) 18%

c) 20%

d) 30%

59. Matthew sells his home to Sam. Who pays the transfer tax?

a) Matthew

b) Sam

c) a and b

d) neither

60. An investor gets a 30-year loan due in 15 years. This is a(n):

a) VA loan

b) package mortgage

c) balloon

d) open-end mortgage

61. In order for Farah, a Virginia real estate broker, to renew her license she must:

a) complete 24 hours of continuing education

b) complete 16 hours of continuing education

c) complete 20 hours of continuing education

d) retake the real estate exam

62. The most probable price that an informed purchaser might pay is the:

a) sales price

b) broker price opinion

c) market value

d) assessed value

63. A lender prequalifies a couple for a loan amount up to $375,000 with a 3.5% down payment. What booklet must he give them within three days of application?

a) an information booklet prepared by HUD

b) a booklet on the explanation of closing costs

c) Regulation Z booklet

d) HUD-1 booklet

64. When a borrower makes a down payment less than 20% and gets an FHA loan, what monthly charge should they expect to be added to their mortgage payment?

a) property taxes

b) funding fee

c) mortgage insurance premium

d) equity loan payment

65._____ backs rural development loans.

a) a life insurance company

b) FHA

c) Freddie Mac

d) Ginnie Mae

66. The sales comparison approach is also known as the:

a) appraisal process

b) market data

c) replacement cost

d) cost

67. "DUST" is a term associated with:

a) licensing

b) title

c) appraisals

d) conformity

68. In Virginia, if there are more homes on the market than buyers, there is:

a) regression

b) more supply than demand

c) substitution

d) law of decreasing return

69. If a three-family home is valued at $769,000 and the cap rate is 9%, what is the annual net operating income?

a) $69,210

b) $85,444

c) $100,000

d) $71,000

70. Tim inherits his family's farm which has suffered years of neglect. He decides to take an equity loan on the property, so his realtor orders an appraisal. While doing the appraisal, the appraiser sees obvious physical deterioration and also notices that a bathroom was never added to the home, it still has an outhouse. The lack of an inside bathroom is a _____.

a) functional obsolescence

b) physical deterioration

c) economic obsolescence

d) accrued depreciation

71. Another name for the Federal Fair Housing Act is _____.

a) Fair Housing

b) Title VIII of the Civil Rights Act of 1968

c) Federal Civil Rights Act of 1866

d) Consumer Protection Law

72. Virginia allows non-residents to hold a real estate license if they:

a) move to Virginia

b) sign a notarized letter appointing a family member as their attorney-in-fact

c) purchase a two-family home and keep the unit as their second residence

d) file a power of attorney appointing the chairman of the board as their attorney-in-fact

73. Each of these is grounds for license suspension or revocation EXCEPT:

a) commingling personal and business funds

b) acting as an undisclosed dual agent

c) owing no fiduciary duties to clients while acting as a facilitator

d) practicing real estate with an inactive license

74. All have right of survivorship EXCEPT:

a) tenancy in common

b) tenancy by entirety

c) joint tenancy

d) none of the above

75. The best form of ownership is:

a) *pur autre vie*

b) leasehold

c) fee simple

d) freehold

76. Mary and John owned their home as joint tenants until Mary died. Which statement is true?

a) John now has to sell his home.

b) If there is a loan on the property, the lender will call the loan due.

c) John will become the sole owner.

d) John will have to move.

77. In Virginia an unlicensed person lists his property for sale stating that he is in fact a licensed agent. What might his fine be?

a) $500

b) $1,500

c) $1,500

d) $20,000

78. A licensed agent who is associated with a brokerage is a(n):

a) broker

b) salesperson

c) processor

d) escrow agent

79. Overlooked by many homeowners, which is NOT a cost of owning a home?

a) repairs

b) interest paid on the mortgage loan

c) personal property taxes

d) maintenance

80. Which is MOST likely to influence a person's decision to purchase a home in a certain location?

a) street signage

b) school ratings

c) high number of planned unit developments

d) loan types

81. The only time a broker can add personal funds to the escrow account is:

a) never

b) to maintain a minimum balance in the escrow account

c) to purchase investment property using the escrow account

d) if a purchaser asks the broker to hold funds

82. Virginia is a _____ -contract state.

a) 1

b) 2

c) 4

d) 3

83. Mr. and Mrs. Sellers signed the purchase and sale agreement in which they are selling their home to the Buyer family. The Buyers have moved forward in getting all inspections, appraisals, etc., ordered on the property. But the Sellers are now feeling sad and desire to terminate the contract. Which statement is true?

a) they are the owners and maintain the right to terminate the contract at any time

b) they may be forced to sell their home as the contract is legal and binding

c) if they offer to return the Buyers' deposit and pay other incurred expenses the Buyers must accept this and allow them to terminate the contract

d) none of the above are true

84. Which of the following ads will require more disclosures?

a) We have no money down loans

b) VA, FHA and conventional loans offered here

c) APR is 4.5% on a 30-year fixed loan

d) The interest rate is 4.375% per year

85. A missing _____ could cause a home to not pass an FHA inspection.

a) refrigerator

b) freestanding stove

c) cooktop

d) washer/dryer

86. Larry is purchasing a home that has $20,000 in needed repairs but he doesn't have $20,000. What loan is a good option for him?

a) FHA 203(b)

b) FHA 203(k)

c) FHA 203(c)

d) FHA

87. The minimum age in Virginia to receive a salesperson's license is:

a) 21

b) 25

c) 16

d) 18

88. In Virginia when an agent provides information that another agent has requested, this term is known as:

a) cooperate

b) equity share

c) co-broker

d) commission split

89. In Virginia, a salesperson can work as a(n):

a) employee of the broker

b) independent contractor under the broker

c) a or b

d) neither

90. A Virginia law that protects consumers is:

a) Commonwealth Regulations 123

b) Virginia Lemon Law

c) Consumer credit laws

d) Uniform Deceptive Trade Practices Act

91. Jim does a lot of home improvement projects, so he built a shed on his neighbor Jerry's land. Jim has used this shed continuously for over 20 years. Jim can pursue a claim of _____ in order to gain title the property.

a) adverse possession

b) eminent domain

c) servient tenement

d) concurrent ownership

92. An ad reads "2-story traditional 1,500 square foot home in Woodbridge, Virginia for sale. Asking $423,000. Please call Rhonda at 857-455-8234." From a legal perspective, the ad is missing:

a) Rhonda's last name

b) Rhonda disclosing that she is a broker

c) number of bedrooms and bathrooms

d) Rhonda disclosing her brokerage's name and that she is a licensed broker

93. What is a broker's commission fee percent if she sells a building for $673,225 and her fee earned is $16,830.62?

a) 2.5%

b) 6.5%

c) 3.5 %

d) 4.0%

94. Another name for loan fees is:

a) application fee

b) credit report fee

c) discount points

d) broker's fees

95. The Federal Civil Rights Act was passed in:

a) 1968

b) 1866

c) 1868

d) 1986

96. The _____ sets the minimum requirements for appraisals.

a) RESPA

b) MLS

c) TILA

d) USPAP

97. A section is:

a) 2 square miles

b) a city block

c) 27,878,400 square feet

d) 43,560 acres

98. After what year did Virginia mandate that all new or rehabbed four-family homes or larger first floor units be disability accessible?

a) 1968

b) 1991

c) 2002

d) 1986

99. Which is not covered under the Fair Housing laws?

a) an SFR that is corporate owned

b) elderly housing that meets certain Department of Housing and Urban Development guidelines

c) a two-to-four-unit dwelling that is not owner occupied

d) a home owned by an individual who owns more than three properties

100. Within a three-year period, an owner has been found guilty of sending discriminatory letters to his tenants. The owner may have to pay civil penalties up to _____ if this is his first offense:

a) $25,000

b) $10,000

c) $50,000

d) $20,000

Real Estate Sales Exam I Answers

1. b. The couple (owner) is conveying title to the real property.

2. a. 1 acre = 43,560 square feet   43,560 square feet x .25 = 10,890 square feet

3. d. None of the above. The property is a primary residence which has been lived in at least two of the most recent five years and then sold at a gain of less than $500,000.

4. d. The effective gross amount is $4,500 + $150 (the sum of all income generated.)

5. a. The transaction is "non-arm's length" because they are related.

6. d. A breach of contract occurs when one of the parties does not follow through with their end of the contract. The party that did not break the contract can sue for damages.

7. b. Sub-agency requires that the listing broker obtain written permission from the seller and that the fiduciary duties are to the seller.

8. a. To eliminate the mortgage insurance premium, the loan-to-value must be below 80%.

9. a. A contract is defined as an agreement between two or more persons or entities and can be written or oral.

10. a. This is not an arm's length transaction because the brother and sister are related; therefore, the sold price cannot be included with arm's length sales comps.

11. c. Emblements are crops that are annually cultivated.

12. b. Each spouse has equal interest in property acquired during marriage.

13. c. Because the borrower has transferred the property, the lender is allowed to demand full payment.

14. c. In Virginia the agent cannot recommend an inspector.

15. d. Fannie Mae and Freddie Mac purchase conventional loans.

16. b. Processors prepare the loan package for the underwriter.

17. b. Mortgage brokers bring borrowers together with lenders.

18. a. The first step to obtaining home loan financing is to submit the application.

19. c. VA loans offer 100% financing and include a funding fee.

20. b. Shared equity is when the lender offers a low interest rate in exchange for a portion of the equity.

21. c. This contract was written with a financing contingency in which the purchaser was given a date by which to secure financing.

22. a. The property manager is required to make and keep a copy of collected funds for three years.

23. d. Under the Lead Paint Law, the buyer gets 10 days to test for evidence of lead paint.

24. d. There are two members who are not real estate professionals. Their role is to represent the public.

25. b. The cost approach is used when the appraiser has difficulty finding comps.

26. a. FNMA purchases conventional loans.

27. a. The new mortgage will include the remaining balance on the existing first mortgage.

28. d. The lender must do an appraisal, ensure the borrower has means to repay the mortgage and meet the lender's credit score.

29. b. Points charged by a lender are to lower the interest rate for the borrower.

30. d. RESPA prohibits several types of payments to persons who did not perform a service.

31. b. The term is for four years.

32. c. The Civil Rights Act of 1866 prohibits discrimination on the basis of race in the sale, lease, or other transfer of real or personal property.

33. b. A HUD-1 is also known as a Uniform Settlement Statement.

34. a. The title insurance companies protect the holder from defects in the title.

35. c. An exclusive right to sell listing allows the broker to receive a commission no matter who sells the property.

36. d. Eminent domain gives the government the right to take private property for public use.

37. c. In a net lease, the tenant pays the maintenance and operating expenses.

38. a. Because he made energy efficient improvements he has weatherized his home.

39. b. The maximum a Virginia landlord can charge a new tenant is first month's rent + second month's rent + security deposit + cost for new keys and lock change. 3 x $923 + $150 = $2,919.

40. c. Subtract the listing broker's commission from the total commission percentage. Then multiply that number by the home sales price. Then multiply that number by the listing broker's split with his agent. 6 - 3.5 = 2.5% x $44,9000 = $11,225 x 55% = $6,174.

41. b. The lender offered only one loan type to homebuyers purchasing in the area which is more than likely a low to moderate income area.

42. d. To be a broker in Virginia she has to pass the test, be at least 18 years old, have a valid salesperson's license, and provide proof that she has been an active salesperson for at least 36 of the last 48 months.

43. a. Real estate licenses are good for two, not four, years in Virginia.

44. a. FHA-insured loans protect the lender in the event the borrower defaults.

45. c. Condos are created under the Virginia Condominium Act which provides a permit for multi-unit buildings to be divided into separate units that can be owned by an individual fee simple estate.

46. d. Non-freehold estates give the holder of the estate the right to occupy the property until the end of the lease.

47. b. Notice to Quit forms are used to tell the tenant to comply with the terms of the lease or leave the premises.

48. a. Short sale is when the bank gives the homeowner permission to sell the home when they owe more than it is worth.

49. d. "OLD CAR" is an acronym used to remember the agent's fiduciary duties to their client.

50. c. In a dual agency, the broker represents both parties in a transaction.

51. d. A broker cannot mix business and personal funds, refuse to pay a client his escrow funds when requested or hold out on paying his sales agent.

52. c. When no heirs can be found, the state can lay claim to the property.

53. a. A joint tenant can transfer title but the new owner becomes a tenant in common with the other joint tenants. For joint tenancy to be valid everyone has to go on title at the same time.

54. d. A purchase money mortgage is when the seller holds the financing for the borrower.

55. b. Price per square foot is found by dividing the price by the square feet. $328,000/2980 = $110.

56. d. Multiply the lot dimensions 378 x 296 = 111,888 square feet. Determine how many acres the lot is. An acre is 43,560 square feet; therefore, divide 111,888/ 43,560 = 2.57 acres. Divide the cost of $198,000 by 2.57 = $77,042.

57. c. New landlord leases property back to the tenant.

58. a. Divide the down payment by the sales price. $104,250/$417,000 = .25 or 25%.

59. a. The Commonwealth of Virginia charges tax stamps whenever real property changes hands and this expense is paid by the seller at closing.

60. c. In a balloon mortgage the final lump sum is due on the balloon termination date.

61. a. A broker must take 24 hours of continuing education classes within two years to renew their license.

62. c. Market value is the most probable price that an informed buyer will pay.

63. a. Per RESPA, a lender or mortgage broker must give a borrower a copy of a HUD-prepared information booklet within three days of application.

64. c. FHA provides mortgage insurance to protect the lender in case of default and the borrower pays a monthly fee along with their mortgage payment.

65. d. The Government National Mortgage Association (Ginnie Mae) is a major purchaser of government-backed mortgage loans.

66. b. The market data approach is also known as the comparison approach.

67. c. DUST is an acronym for the elements that establish value and is associated with appraisals.

Demand for the type of property

Utility (desirable use) the property offers

Scarcity of properties available

Transferability of property to a new owner

68. b. There's a larger inventory of homes than there are buyers.

69. a. Value x Cap rate = Net Operating Income

   769,000 x .09 = 69,210

70. a. Functional obsolescence highlights features that are no longer considered desirable.

71. b. The Federal Fair Housing Act broadened the prohibitions against discrimination in housing to include sex, race, color, religion, national origin, disability, and familial status in connection with the sale or rental of housing.

72. d. Virginia allows non-residents to hold a real estate license if they file a power of attorney appointing the Chairman of the Board as their attorney-in-fact for legal issues relating to that individual.

73. c. A facilitator (non-agent) owes no fiduciary duties to clients.

74. a. Tenancy in common does not have right of survivorship. Tenancy by entirety is a form of joint tenancy and has right of survivorship, as does joint tenancy.

75. c. Fee simple is a type of freehold estate and is the best form of ownership because the owner has the right to occupy or rent the property, to sell or transfer its ownership, to build on it and mine it for minerals, and to restrict or allow the use of the property to others.

76. c. Joint tenancy includes the right of survivorship; the surviving co-owners share equally in the deceased owner's interest.

77. a. The Virginia fine for performing real estate business without a license is $500.

78. b. A licensed agent who is associated with a brokerage is a salesperson.

79. c. Personal property taxes are taxes on personal property not real property.

80. b. School ratings can influence whether a person purchases in a certain area.

81. b. A broker can mix business and personal funds if the broker needs to add funds to maintain a minimum balance in the escrow account.

82. a. Virginia is a one-contract state. The Purchase and Sale Agreement outlines the entire transaction.

83. b. Because the contract is legal and binding, if the Sellers don't move forward, they will be in breach of contract and the Buyers can sue for specific performance.

84. a. The ad should disclose the loan amount, down payment, APR, and terms of repayment.

85. c. FHA minimum property guidelines state that the home must be delivered in safe, secure and sound condition. A freestanding stove could be considered personal property, but a cooktop (because it is attached) is a part of the home.

86. b. FHA 203(k) is FHA's Rehabilitation Loan Insurance Program.

87. d. Virginia's minimum age for a real estate license is 18.

88. a. In real estate when an agent provides information that another agent has requested, this is to cooperate.

89. c. The agent can work as an independent contractor or as an employee.

90. d. The Virginia Uniform Deceptive Trade Practices Act prohibits unfair and deceptive trade practices and real estate agents and brokers are subject to this.

91. a. Adverse possession is a method of acquiring title to another person's property through court action after continuous use for over 15 years in Virginia.

92. d. The broker must disclose her name and that she is a licensed broker.

93. a. Divide the total commission earned by the sales price. $16830.62/$673,225 = .025 x 100 = 2.5%.

94. c. Discount points are loan fees that the buyer can pay to get a lower interest rate.

95. b. The Federal Civil Rights Act was passed in 1866 to prohibit discrimination on the basis of race.

96. d. The Uniform Standards of Professional Appraisal Practice (USPAP) sets the minimum requirement for appraisals.

97. c. A section is 640 acres. 640 acres x 43,560 square feet per acre = 27,878,400 square feet.

98. b. The Federal Fair Housing Act of 1968 prohibits discrimination against mentally or physically disabled individuals. Then after 1991 it was mandated that all new or rehabbed four-family or larger homes must be designed so the first floor units include disability accessibility.

99. b. The Federal Fair Housing Act does not cover housing for the elderly that meets certain HUD guidelines.

100. b. Under the Federal Fair Housing Act, a person can pay civil penalties up to $10,000 for the first offense.

Real Estate Sales Exam II

1. My Town Realty gets a listing to sell a home. The broker appoints one of his sales agents (with permission of the sellers), Melissa to represent the sellers. During one of the open houses, a couple comes in and decides to make an offer, so they call the broker at My Town Realty, who then assigns one of his other sales agents, Keith, to represent the buyers. In this case the broker is acting as a:

a) non-agent

b) designated seller's and buyer's agent/dual agent

c) single agent

d) principal agent

2. A buyer secures a first mortgage for $243,750, puts down 15% and the seller carries back 10%. What was the sales price of the home if she paid full asking?

a) $250,000

b) $300,000

c) $375,000

d) $325,000

3. All are true statements regarding appraisal reports EXCEPT?

a) they can be orally delivered

b) they must be delivered on the Uniform Residential Appraisal Report

c) must use guidelines set forth by USPAP

d) they can be delivered in writing

4. Seller competition in the market usually results in:

a) higher home prices

b) lower home prices

c) anticipation

d) progression

5. The disposition, control, right of possession and enjoyment are all:

a) zoning ordinances

b) intangibles

c) corporeal

d) the bundle of rights of ownership

6. All are real property EXCEPT:

a) air rights

b) refrigerator

c) oak tree

d) pond

7. Monica owns a parcel of land. Her tax bill is $1,150. If her tax rate is $2.50 per acre, how many acres is her property?

a) 460 acres

b) 1150 acres

c) 750 acres

d) 115 acres

8. A church, which has 501(c) (3) status is exempt from paying:

a) a mortgage

b) property taxes

c) hazard insurance

d) licensing fees

9. Anthony sells his condo to Michael. Besides getting a certified letter from the condo association, what other certificate must he obtain?

a) insurance

b) 21(e)

c) property tax

d) freehold

10. Matthew decides to purchase a home, so he gives his landlord of two years a 30-day notice. If his security deposit was $1,345 and the bank interest rate (where the landlord held his deposit) was 1%, how much money should he expect back?

a) $1,545.38

b) $1,345

c) $1,358.45

d) $1,435

11. Even though Jennifer's lease ended over a month ago, she has not moved out. What type of tenancy does she now have?

a) tenancy at will

b) tenancy for years

c) tenancy for period to period

d) tenancy at sufferance

12. Realtors are members of the:

a) NAREB

b) NRA

c) NAR

d) REBAC

13. A lender needs to set a listing price on one of their foreclosed homes. They will more than likely order a(n):

a) mortgage payment history

b) appraisal

c) assessed value report

d) BPO

14. Which one is an example of commercial real estate?

a) a 21-unit apartment complex

b) a store for rent

c) a storefront with apartments on the second floor

d) loft apartments

15. Julian refuses to pay his condo association fees; he runs the risk of the association placing a priority lien on his property. This bill is known as the:

a) Priority Lien

b) 6(d) certificate

c) Virginia General Laws 183A

d) Super Lien

16. *Fructus naturales* refers to:

a) real property

b) emblements

c) natural fruit

d) annually cultivated crops

17. An exploration company purchases the rights to any minerals and oil from an owner. The owner now owns all rights EXCEPT the following:

a) subsurface

b) water

c) air

d) surface

18. In Virginia a manufactured home is proven by:

a) mortgage deed

b) mortgage note

c) bill of sale

d) purchase contract

19. Cheri was so happy when she received checks from her lender that she could use to pay her contractor.   She had taken out a(n) _____mortgage.

a) equity

b) land sales

c) purchase money mortgage

d) primary

20. Bill negotiated the lease for his new apartment on the phone and told the landlord that he could sign the lease and meet in person within three days. However, Bill experienced an emergency and had to fly out of town right away, so he told his twin brother Tom to meet the landlord and sign the lease for him. The lease is:

a) valid

b) void

c) voidable

d) illegal

21. In two days, Jackie was anticipating going to her home loan closing, but instead she received a call from her agent that the home had an old second lien on it that the seller said he had paid off. What term best describes the title?

a) the title is free and clear

b) the title is encumbered

c) the title is vested

d) the title is clouded

22. Due to the economy and a loss of jobs in the area, home prices have fallen by 46% and are now valued at about $372,000. Based on the information, what was the average home price before the values fell?

a) $866,000

b) $689,000

c) $668,000

d) $888,888

23. Janet's landlord locked her out of the building she lives in Roanoke, Virginia. She decides that she wants to file a lawsuit against him but finds that he has filed bankruptcy. She must file her case with which court?

a) Janet cannot file a lawsuit; she must go before the bankruptcy court

b) Judicial

c) Housing

d) District

24. A couple, who had their home listed with Any Town Brokerage, hosted a Christmas party. One of the guests from the party loved the home and came back over to ask them several questions about the house and to get a formal tour. He ended up purchasing the home and the sellers did not have to pay Any Town Brokerage any commission. What type of listing did they have with Any Town?

a) dual

b) net

c) open

d) exclusive agency

25. An apartment purchaser receives shares and a limited partnership. What type of apartment was purchased?

a) condo

b) cooperative

c) multi unit

d) three-family home

26. Seventeen-year-old Arthur, a college student, is told by a landlord that he is too young to rent one of his apartments. Which Virginia state law might the landlord be violating?

a) VRLTA

b) Equal Housing Act

c) Fair Housing Act

d) Uniform Deceptive Trade Practices Act

27. Balance contributes to value when:

a) there is homogeneity in a neighborhood

b) there are diverse land uses

c) there is conformity

d) there is regression

28. If an agent is found to have violated Virginia fair housing laws, he may be required to pay damages up to _____ times those incurred by the victim.

a) 3

b) 120

c) 30

d) 9

29. Mrs. Tenant vacated her apartment because her landlord turned off the water. This was a(n):

a) adverse eviction

b) lease back

c) constructive eviction

d) contractual eviction

30. In a 99-year lease, the buyer typically receives all bundle of rights EXCEPT:

a) enjoyment

b) possession

c) control of use

d) none of the above

31. Missy paid her landlord the first month's rent and a security deposit. What does Virginia state law mandate that he give her?

a) thank you letter

b) keys immediately

c) list of tenant rules

d) receipt

32. How long must receipts for rental payments, including canceled checks or money orders, be kept by a broker in Virginia?

a) 30 days past the end of the lease

b) 3 years

c) 1 year

d) 10 years past the termination of the lease

33. In Virginia, what type of tenancy does a tenant who lives in public housing have if they have additional tenant protections?

a) tenant at will

b) tenant with written lease

c) tenant by regulation

d) tenant at sufferance

34. Another name for a tenant at will is _____.

a) yearly lease

b) common tenancy

c) sublease

d) month to month

35. In a Virginia mobile home park transaction, if the landlord acts as the seller's sales agent, the landlord's fee cannot exceed _____%.

a) 6

b) 3.5

c) 5

d) 10

36. The _____ requires that all Purchase and Sale Agreements must be in writing.

a) National Association of Realtors

b) Virginia Statute of Frauds

c) US Department of Housing and Urban Development

d) Virginia License Law

37. A seller will pay 3% in closing cost. If the sales price is $378,499 and the buyer is putting down a 20% down payment, which is the amount paid by the seller?

a) $2,270

b) $9,084

c) $3,000

d) $11,355

38. Virginia property managers must have a:

a) broker's license

b) two-year degree

c) real estate salesperson's license

d) none of the above

39. Mike and Dana are renting a unit in their 1946 two-family home to a couple with a five-year-old child. What must they (Mike and Dana) do in accordance to the Lead Law?

a) de-lead

b) give the new tenants a Lead Paint Notice

c) have the tenants sign an escalation lease

d) provide the tenants a stock certificate

40. Stan and his business partner decide to sell their four-unit property. They find another four-unit property in a town closer to where they live which will make it easier to manage. What technique can they use that may ease their current income tax burden from the sale?

a) 1031 exchange

b) owner financing

c) hard money loan

d) equity loan

41. If you are a tenant in a property that has been foreclosed, your tenancy will:

a) terminate and you must immediately move out

b) automatically convert to a written lease with the lender

c) automatically turn into a tenancy at will

d) turn into an option to purchase

42. Sharon was told that her front and back end numbers were 48/55 and that she did not qualify for a home loan at this time. These are called _____.

a) LTV

b) qualifying ratios

c) cost per unit

d) income to debt ratios

43. Farmer Jedd has _____ rights in that he is able to allow his horses to drink from the river next to his property.

a) mineral

b) air and surface

c) littoral

d) riparian

44. In Virginia, when two people are co-owners on a property, the three types of ownership are:

a) tenancy in common, tenancy in sufferance, and tenancy as written

b) joint tenancy, tenancy at will, and tenancy in common

c) tenancy by the entirety, tenancy in common, and joint tenancy

d) tenancy in common, tenancy by the entirety and tenancy in sufferance

45. An agent lost her wallet with her real estate license. In order to get a duplicate, she must_____.

a) complete the change of name form on the Board's website

b) misplaced license form

c) retake the test

d) only send in the applicable fee, no form is needed.

46. Mitzi is a licensed agent but no longer wishes to perform real estate. The only thing she needs to do is:

a) send a resignation letter to her broker

b) send a resignation letter to the Board

c) not pay the renewal fee

d) tell the Board members in person when they have a meeting

47. In Virginia, a first-time homebuyer is someone who hasn't owned a property for _____ years.

a) 4

b) 5

c) never owned a home

d) 3

48. The Taxpayer Relief Act was passed in:

a) 1997

b) 1986

c) 1977

d) 2001

49. Flood insurance is:

a) always optional

b) required in certain areas

c) automatically included in the hazard insurance policy

d) only available to homeowners purchasing properties financed by rural housing

50. Patty has gotten a loan pre-approval from Conservative Trust Bank. More than likely, her housing expense ratio does not exceed _____ percent.

a) 38

b) 20

c) 28

d) 33

51. For keeping real estate contracts in Virginia, _____ year(s) is the Contract Law Statute of Limitations.

a) 1

b) 3

c) 6

d) 8

52. Under the cost approach, the formula for determining value is:

a) Replacement or reproduction cost – Accrued Depreciation + Land Value = Value

b) Accrued Depreciation – Replacement or reproduction cost + Land Value = Value

c) Replacement or reproduction cost + Accrued Depreciation – Land Value = Value

d) Replacement or reproduction cost + Land Value – Accrued Depreciation = Value

53. All are examples of a protected class EXCEPT:

a) children

b) veterans

c) elderly

d) all of the above

54. A broker told an elderly couple that for $3,000 she could help them get their loan modified to a more affordable payment, but after the couple gave her the money she disappeared. What Virginia law has the broker violated?

a) The Federal Civil Rights Act

b) The Virginia General Law Chapter 151B

c) Virginia Lead Paint Law

d) Virginia Consumer Protection Law (Chapter 93A)

55. The _____ pledges the property as collateral.

a) mortgage lien

b) mortgage deed

c) mortgage note

d) collateralization note

56. Land, "bundle of legal rights," and permanent, man-made additions are:

a) personal property

b) emblements

c) real property

d) real estate

57. Lisa and Mike are remodeling their home. The contractor unloads a truckload of drywall and tile in front of their house. The delivered items are:

a) personal property

b) encumbrances

c) real property

d) real estate

58. Which is NOT one of the "bundle of rights"?

a) right to transfer the home to a relative

b) right to live in the home

c) right to refuse entry into the home

d) right to run a neighborhood casino

59. Which economic characteristic of real estate best represents the following example? Two identical homes built by the same developer are located on Milford Street, which is a street that separates two cities, Old City and New City.   House A is in New City and sits on the west side of the street and House B sits on the east side of the street and is in Old City. Because it is a newer area, homeowners believe that the school district in New City is better than Old City.

a) relative scarcity

b) area preference

c) supply and demand

d) improvements

60. A granddaughter inherited a home worth about $225,000 that her grandparents lived in for 50 years. This home had a great deal of sentimental value to her so because of this she decided to remodel the home to her taste, which costs her well over $380,000 in remodeling costs. While the home's value did increase to $300,000, the appraiser did tell her that she over-improved the home for that neighborhood. What type of value does this home now have?

a) objective

b) indestructible

c) subjective

d) immobility

61. In Virginia a brokerage can exist under a temporary broker's license without examination when:

a) the broker travels out of the country

b) the broker decides to appoint one of his agents as a broker

c) the broker is late in completing his continuing education and paying the renewal fee

d) the broker of record passes away

62. A Virginia broker acting on behalf of a developer of an out of state real estate development has to notify the Board in writing of their status within _____ days of accepting the client.

a) 7

b) 2

c) 5

d) 10

63. Who can issue a junior mortgage?

a) Freddie Mac

b) the VA

c) the seller

d) RHS

64. Kelley, Marvin and Andrea are joint tenants. When Andrea dies, Kelley and Marvin remain as joint tenants. When Marvin dies, Kelley now holds title as a sole owner. Kelley now holds title in _____.

a) common

b) severalty

c) entirety

d) life estate

65. Greg has an oceanfront property where he is able to freely enjoy the ocean at any time. He has _____ rights.

a) bundle of rights

b) alluvion

c) riparian

d) littoral

66. A _____ is divided into 36 sections.

a) city

b) township

c) commonwealth

d) acre

67. In a deed, *et ux* means:

a) and wife

b) everyone

c) and others

d) and husband

68. Abraham bought a property and later learned that his great grandfather's father may have owned that property. What can he order that will show the property ownership history?

a) deed of trust

b) legal description

c) certificate of title

d) chain of title

69. A chattel mortgage would more than likely be used in a transaction with all of the following EXCEPT:

a) car

b) furniture

c) single family residence

d) mobile home

70. A developer plans to build a new subdivision that is pedestrian friendly. The homes will be on small lots, but the community will have several "green" areas with parks and common areas for the residents. This type of design is known as _____.

a) communal property

b) clustering

c) commingling

d) canvassing

71. Mrs. James' husband passed away about six months ago and because she is on fixed income she is finding it difficult to meet all of her expenses due to her husband's remaining medical bills. Because she owns her home free and clear and she would like to remain in it, what loan product might be a good option for her?

a) junior mortgage

b) HELOC

c) primary mortgage

d) HECM

72. Which is NOT a method used to satisfy the requirement for legal description in a deed?

a) the Torrens System

b) the metes and bounds system

c) the lot and block system

d) the government survey system

73. Juliet has lived in her apartment for four months and loves it. Because summer is approaching and she does not have air conditioning, she's decided to replace her dining room lighting fixture with a ceiling fan. The ceiling fan will now be:

a) a riparian right

b) an easement

c) real property

d) personal property

74. A hardship associated with acquiring rental property is:

a) the law of increasing returns

b) lack of reserves

c) negative amortization

d) redlining

75. A broker's license is NOT required:

a) when an individual sells his candy store business to another individual

b) when he offers to list real property for sale

c) when he offers to sell his parents' home

d) in exchange for one month's rent, negotiate the rental of real estate for another individual

76. The ADA is the:

a) American Disabled Vets Act

b) American Disposition of Realty Act

c) American Disposal Act

d) Americans with Disabilities Act

77.   Misty works as a sales agent under Real Time Realty in which she is an independent contractor. She should expect all of the following EXCEPT:

a) to assume responsibility for paying her own income tax

b) to compensated on production

c) to receive employee benefits from the broker

d) that she and the broker will have a written contract

78. Manny and Lisa purchased their home six years ago for $325,000 where they put down 10%. Their interest rate was 6.5% and after making 72 monthly payments, their loan balance was $268,901.06. Assuming the current market value and the sales price are the same, how much equity does the homeowner have?

a) $32,500

b) $56,098.94

c) $29,200

d) none of the above

79. Every homeowner is entitled to the following income tax deductions EXCEPT:

a) loan interest on second homes

b) property taxes

c) discount points

d) penalty-free withdrawals up to $10,000 from an IRA

80. Byron, a first time homebuyer, bought his home for $72,500 with an FHA loan. The contract was executed April 28th, 2010. Because he had a 60-day escrow, he finally got his keys on June 30th, 2010. How much tax credit money should he expect to get back if he has no other tax liabilities?

a) $7,250

b) $500

c) $8,000

d) $7,500

81. Which physical characteristic of real estate best describes the following: two parcels of land are not identical:

a) homogeneity

b) immobility

c) non-homogeneity

d) a physical characteristic of land

82. All are uses of real property EXCEPT:

a) residential

b) grazing cattle

c) cemetery

d) all of the above

83. The first real estate license law was passed in _____ in 1919.

a) Virginia

b) New York

c) California

d) Texas

84. A cookie shop owner needs to move to a larger location. When he removed the oven, he repaired the holes from the bolts on the walls and the floors. The oven was a(n):

a) fixture

b) trade fixture

c) real property

d) appurtenance

85. The section on the 1003 that deals with the race or ethnicity and sex of an application is data collected under the:

a) Home Mortgage Disclosure Act

b) Community Redevelopment Act

c) Fair Housing Act

c) Federal Civil Rights Act

86. Broker Connie says the following phrases to her clients, "Better sell the house before too many of them move in the neighborhood," "There goes the neighborhood." These are examples of:

a) redlining

b) steering

c) blockbusting

d) commingling

87. Randy meets with loan officer Jackie so she can prequalify him for a loan. After talking with Randy she learns that he is unmarried and decides to halt the application process. Randy calls her several times only to receive a voicemail. Since it appears as though Jackie is discriminating against Randy on the basis of marital status, what law is she violating?

a) The Civil Rights Act of 1964

b) The ADA

c) The Federal Fair Housing Act of 1866

d) ECOA

88. Which is NOT a purpose of the License Law?

a) raise revenue

b) to protect the public from incompetent brokers

c) prescribe minimum standards for licensing brokers

d) protect licensed brokers and salespersons from unfair or improper competition

89. Which is the best acronym to help in remembering the four government powers?

a) DUST

b) OLD CAR

c) PETE

d) PPEDTE

90. Ms. Mary owned the land adjacent to her church and decided to grant it to the church so long as it is used to build a recreation center for the church's youth. This type of estate is known as:

a) fee simple

b) determinable fee

c) legal fee

d) conventional life estate

91. Sonja gave her $3,500 earnest money deposit to her sales agent. What should her sales agent do next?

a) deposit the check in his (sales agents) personal checking account

b) give the check to the office's transaction coordinator who will then put the check in the company's escrow account

c) cash the check and give Sonja a receipt

d) give the check to the office's transaction coordinator who will then place the check in file folder with Sonja's name on it along with the contract and store them safely in the file cabinet

92. Johnny and Donna visit a new home development and fall in love with the model homes. All of the homes in this subdivision will only have one level. After picking a floor plan they like, they ask the sales agent what the cost would be to add a second story media room and bathroom. The sales agent advises the couple that the developers have created a _____ _____ that does not permit two-story homes in the subdivision.

a) planning and zoning law

b) inverse condemnation

c) public control

d) deed restriction

93. Ted received a letter stating that the lender had obtained a deficiency judgment against him. Which scenario below best fits what has happened to Ted?

a) One of his creditors from a credit card put his account in collections then filed a judgment against him.

b) The home was sold in an auction for the amount he owed, but because there were no funds to pay the agents the lenders paid it and are now suing Ted for the deficiency.

c) Ted's loan balance and fees were more than the home sold for at foreclosure sale; therefore, the lender will claim Ted's other assets in order to satisfy the indebtedness.

d) none of the above

94. When working on behalf of a seller or buyer, an agent must exhibit good business judgment, trust and honesty. This is because of their _____ _____.

a) fiduciary relationship

b) faithful performance

c) implied authority

d) special agent

95. Keith is selling his five-unit complex. He should be prepared to bring all documents below EXCEPT:

a) tax returns

b) lease agreements

c) maintenance contracts

d) estoppels letters from the tenants

96. Baker and Johnson Partnership decides to sell off some of its real estate. If the partners hold title as tenants in common, which signatures will be required to convey the real estate?

a) Only one signature is required since it is a partnership.

b) Since each partner holds title, they will each have to sign.

c) They can sign with a stamp in the name of their partnership.

d) Whenever a partnership sells real estate, only two signatures are required no matter how many partners there are.

97. Theron and Perry are neighbors. Theron builds a fence in which two feet of it extends into Perry's property. The fence is an example of a(n):

a) eminent domain

b) encumbrance

c) encroachment

d) easement by necessity

98. A couple residing in a community property state have been married for five years. During the marriage, the wife's grandfather decides to give each grandchild their inheritance, which is one of his income producing properties. The property is _____ of the wife.

a) community property

b) sole proprietorship

c) part of a land trust

d) separate property

99. Real estate ownership by a corporation is a:

a) tenancy in sufferance

b) tenancy in severalty

c) joint tenancy

d) none of the above as corporations can't own real estate

100. Barbara has been pre-approved for a maximum purchase price of $318,000 based on 90% LTV. What will her down payment need to be?

a) $10,000

b) $6,400

c) $32,000

d) $23,000

Real Estate Sales Exam II Answers

1. b. Designated buyer's and seller's agent is an agent who represents their client and owes fiduciary duties to their client and with the client's permission, can be designated by another agent. When the appointing agent designates another agent in the office to represent the other party to the transaction, the broker will also be a dual agent.

2. d. First, we need to establish that the borrower's down payment and the seller carry back can be added together and treated like it is the borrower's down payment. Second, find the loan to value (LTV) which is 100 – 25 = 75% or .75 Since we are given the loan amount and now have the LTV we can solve for the sales price: $243,750/.75 = $325,000.

3. b. The appraisal can be oral or written.

4. b. When sellers are competing there is a lot of supply in the market which drives home prices down.

5. d. The bundle of rights are the property rights which include the right of possession, control, enjoyment and disposition.

6. b. The refrigerator is not attached to the house. The owner can take this with him therefore it is personal property.

7. a. Monica's property is 460 acres. To calculate, divide the total tax bill by the per-acre rate: x = ($1,150)/ (2.50) = 460.

8. b. Nonprofits are exempt from paying property taxes.

9. b. Anthony must provide an insurance certificate showing the new owner and his mortgage holder will be covered under the condominium master insurance policy in order to transfer the property, in Virginia.

10. c. In Virginia, the landlord is to give the tenant the interest he earned in the bank on the deposit.

11. a. Tenancy at will is a lease without a termination date

12. c. National Association of Realtors

13. d. BPO or broker price opinion is when the mortgage holder gets a broker's opinion of value based on a competitive market analysis.

14. b. Commercial property is used to produce income.

15. d. The Super Lien Bill gives the association the right to impose a priority lien.

16. a. Citrus fruit, apples, berries and grapes are considered to be *fructus naturales.* They remain with the real property.

17. a. Subsurface rights are rights below the earth's surface.

18. c. Manufactured homes are considered personal property as most are not permanently affixed.

19. a. Equity mortgage is where the homeowner takes out a portion of the equity on their property and often times lenders will send the borrower checks.

20. c. A voidable contract binds one party but not the other.

21. d. Clouded title is any document, claim, unreleased lien that may impair the title to real property or make the title doubtful.

22. b. First we need to find what percentage of the earlier values is the current value. This is 100 - 46 = 54% or .54. $372,000/.54 = $688,889.

23. a. In Virginia if the landlord has filed bankruptcy, the tenant must go before the bankruptcy court.

24. d. An exclusive agency listing means that only one listing broker represents the seller. The seller retains the right to sell the property on his own without paying a commission.

25. b. Cooperatives are apartments owned by a corporation that holds title to the entire cooperative property.

26. c. The Virginia Fair Housing Act prohibits discrimination on several protected classes in two different categories. Age is in category one.

27. b. Balance is when a neighborhood or town has several different types of land uses.

28. a. An agent may be required to pay up to triple damages if he or she is found to have violated Virginia Fair Housing laws.

29. c. Constructive eviction is when a landlord has rendered a property uninhabitable and the tenant moves out.

30. b. In a 99-year lease the buyer does not have full ownership.

31. d. When a tenant pays fees to a landlord, the landlord must give the tenant a receipt.

32. a. In Virginia, brokers must maintain receipts of rental payments for three years.

33. c. Tenants who live in public housing may have additional protections.

34. d. Tenancy at will is a lease without a termination date.

35. d. The maximum fee the landlord of a mobile park can charge if he acts as the seller's agent is 10%.

36. b. The Virginia Statute of Frauds requires that all Purchase and Sale Agreements must be in writing.

37. d. Closing Cost can be found by multiplying the sales price by the closing cost percent. $378,499 x .03 = $11,355.

38. d. Virginia property managers are not required to have any type of license or degree.

39. b. According to the Lead Paint Law, along with giving the new tenants a Lead Paint Notification and Tenant Certification Form, because the new tenants have a child under six, Mike and Dana must de-lead the property.

40. a. By using the 1031 exchange, they can defer the income tax on their gain until a future date.

41. c. Turn into a tenancy at will with the new owner.

42. b. Qualifying ratios are calculations to determine whether a borrower can qualify for a mortgage.

43. d. Riparian rights are the rights of a landowner whose property is adjacent to a flowing waterway to use the water.

44. c. There are three types of tenancy for co-owners in Virginia: tenancy by the entirety, tenancy in common, and joint tenancy.

45. a. The Change of Name or Request for Duplicate License form located on the Board's website under the Applications and Forms link and send in the applicable fee.

46. c. The Board will make her license inactive if she doesn't pay the renewal fee.

47. d. First-time homebuyers in most states are individuals who have not owned a home in the last two to three years.

48. a. The Taxpayer Relief Act was enacted August 5, 1997.

49. b. Flood insurance may be required if any part of the property is in a flood zone.

50. c. The housing ratio is the front end or housing expense and the back end ratio is the total debt ratio. Conservative lenders tend to use more conservative ratios.

51. c. Under the Virginia Contract Law Statute of Limitations, real estate contracts must be kept for 6 years.

52. a. The formula for determining value: Replacement or reproduction cost - accrued depreciation + land value = value

53. d. A protected class is any group of people designated by HUD.

54. d. The Virginia Consumer Protection Law (Chapter 93A) prohibits unfair and deceptive trade practices.

55. b. The mortgage deed pledges the property as collateral.

56. c. Real property is real estate plus bundle of legal rights.

57. a. Personal property is moveable.

58. d. Illegal purpose uses are not included in the "bundle of rights."

59. b. The economic characteristics of Real Estate are relative scarcity, improvements, permanence of investment and area preference.

60. c. Subjective value is affected by the relative worth someone places on a specific item.

61. d. The Board can, upon application, issue a temporary license without examination to the broker's designated individual or legal representative.

62. a. A broker acting on behalf of an out-of-state developer must notify the Board within seven days of accepting the client.

63. c. The seller can offer to carry back a second mortgage.

64. b. Estate in severalty is sole ownership.

65. d. When a landowner's property borders a large non-flowing body of water such as an ocean, the landowner's right to enjoy the water is a littoral right

66. b. A township is divided into 36 sections.

67. a. Abbreviation for Latin term *et uxor* meaning wife.

68. d. A chain of title is a recorded history of conveyances on a particular property.

69. c. A chattel mortgage is used with personal or moveable property.

70. b. Clustering is when a developer groups home sites on smaller lots and leaves the remaining land for use as common area.

71. d. A home equity conversion mortgage is another name for a reverse mortgage. This type of mortgage allows an elderly person to remain in their home in which the equity is converted to cash for the homeowner.

72. a. The Torrens System facilitates registering title to land with a public authority.

73. c. The ceiling fan became real property once it got attached to the ceiling.

74. b. Most lenders require three to six months of reserves of the PITI payment when purchasing income property which often creates a barrier to entry.

75. a. A license is not required when an individual sells his own business.

76. d. Americans with Disabilities Act

77. c. A broker cannot offer employee benefits to her independent contractors.

78. b. $325,000 - $268,901.06 = $56,098.94

79. d. Only first-time homebuyers can withdraw penalty-free up to $10,000 from their IRA.

80. a. The tax credit was worth 10% of the purchase price.

81. c. No two pieces of land are ever exactly alike.

82. d. All are uses of real property.

83. c. California

84. b. The oven was a trade fixture and because he returned the walls and the floors to their original condition it can be considered personal property.

85. a. The Home Mortgage Disclosure Act (HMDA) requires mortgage lenders to collect and report data to assist in identifying possible discriminatory lending practices.

86. c. Blockbusting is the illegal act of convincing homeowners to sell their properties by suggesting that a protected class is moving into the neighborhood.

87. d. The Equal Credit Opportunity Act prohibits lenders from discriminating against credit applicants on the basis of race, color, religion, national origin, sex, marital status, age or dependence on public assistance.

88. a. The License Law was not enacted to raise revenue.

89. c. The four government powers are PETE: **P**olice Power, **E**minent Domain, **T**axation, and **E**scheat

90. b. This is a determinable fee estate in which the estate will come to an end immediately if the specified purpose ceases.

91. b. All earnest deposits must be held in the company's escrow account.

92. d. Deed restrictions can control from what can be parked in a driveway to what exterior color the homes can be.

93. c. When the proceeds of the foreclosure sale do not cover what is owed, the lender may claim other assets to satisfy the indebtedness.

94. a. A fiduciary relationship requires that an agent exhibit trust, honesty and good business judgment when working on behalf of the principal.

95. a. He does not have to supply his tax returns.

96. b. Each partner will have to sign since they all hold title.

97. c. The fence is an encroachment because it invades the neighbor's property.

98. d. Once the grandfather conveys the property to her it is separate property.

99. b. Because a corporation is a legal entity, corporate real estate ownership is held as tenancy in severalty.

100. c. The down payment is 100 – 90 = 10%   10% of $318,000 = $31,800 or $32,000.

Real Estate Sales Exam III

1. What is the transfer tax the seller will pay in Virginia if he sells his home for $428,000?

a) $0

b) $4,820

c) $1284.33

d) $428

2. Wendy just got her salesperson's license in Virginia. How many continuing education hours does she have to take in the first two years?

a) 30

b) 24

c) 180

d) 16

3. Virginia has reciprocity agreements with _____ states.

a) 49

b) 23

c) 13

d) 10

4. Virginia exempts four groups from paying property tax. They are:

a) disabled, blind, veterans, and elderly

b) surviving spouse and children, elderly, blind, veterans

c) surviving spouse and children, disabled, elderly, veterans

d) elderly, disabled, blind surviving spouse, and children

5. Arthur, the owner of three two-family homes, decides to enlist the help of a property management company to aid him in managing the properties. What type of contract will he have with the property manager?

a) a multiple listing agreement

b) a rental agreement

c) a management agreement

d) a multiple use agreement

6. The Federal Reserve Board's Regulation B implements _____.

a) Equal Credit Opportunity Act

b) Truth in Lending

c) RESPA

d) Home Mortgage Disclosure Act

7. The Hemsley family bought a vacation home in Charlottesville. Their down payment was 40% and they financed the rest. They became the:

a) mortgagee

b) borrower

c) mortgagor

d) lienor

8. Karen, who purchased her apartment in the city for $598,000, tells her friend Samantha that her property tax payment is included in her monthly maintenance fee. Samantha suspects that Karen more than likely purchased a:

a) leasehold

b) PUD

c) condo

d) coop

9. The Stemmons family owns 2,000 acres of land with several stands of trees on the property. Every year they sell the lumber to a timber company. The cut trees are sold as:

a) real property

b) personal property

c) not considered property since they are not a structure

d) an appurtenance

10. Marla, a vendee, has an equitable interest in the property located on 926 Elm Street, Any Town, Any State 12345. In this case Marla is the:

a) seller

b) grantor

c) purchaser

d) grantee

11. Your home has a fence that was installed around 15 years ago and you have lived there for 12 years. You have continuously used your side of the property for six years without any problems. Recently your neighbor had his land surveyed and it appears as though your fence is on his land. In Virginia, if you continue to use the land and your neighbor doesn't say anything, how many years do you have before you can file for adverse possession.

a) 14

b) 1

c) 9

d) 20

12. An option to purchase a home for $325,000 within 120 days was sold to Heather for $9,000. After 60 days the seller accepted an offer from Heather to purchase the home for $305,000. Which is true?

a) Heather violated the agreement.

b) Heather loses her option deposit.

c) Both Heather and the seller are in violation of contract law.

d) Heather could make a new offer for $305,000.

13. A property is worth $214,000 and it has $156,000 in liens tied to it. This difference is known as:

a) the assessed value

b) down payment

c) equity

d) leverage

14. Martha and her daughter made an offer on another home based on their current home selling by a certain date. What type of clause was this?

a) financing

b) contingency

c) recession

d) partial performance

15. An agent meets with a client in their home for the first time and the couple decides to sign the listing agreement authorizing the broker as their listing agent. The agent loves the home and believes it would make a great starter home for Jack, her neighbor's son. The agent holds an open house and receives two offers along with Jack's offer. These offers are all very similar. Then just before she (agent) leaves to present the offers, she gets a new offer which is much better than the current offers. Even though she really wants Jack to get the home, she shows all offers to her client. Which of the six agent responsibilities did the agent demonstrate?

a) loyalty

b) accounting

c) reasonable care

d) confidentiality

16. _____ is when the municipality takes action against a property owner and through the court land process attempts to gain ownership of the property.

a) foreclosure

b) eminent domain

c) taking

d) constructive notice

17. Which is true?

a) FHA is hazard insurance

b) FHA guarantees that the borrower will not default on the loan

c) FHA 203(k) loans are for one-to-four investment properties only

d) FHA insures the lender against borrower default

18. Which contract is voidable?

a) a painter is contracted to paint a home, but two days before he was to begin the job, the home was destroyed by a hurricane.

b) an owner who grows marijuana in his backyard, agrees to sell it to his next door neighbor

c) an older brother who lives with his younger brother because he is mentally challenged and needs supervised care contracts a landscaping company to begin cutting the yard

d) a buyer makes an offer to purchase and includes a financing contingency

19. Real estate often deals with two main types of property. One type is personal property, what is the other type?

a. homeowner property

b. real property

c. building property

d. city-owned property

20. Mr. Sanders and his family bought a property 10 years ago. It has increased in value by 2% every year that he has owned it. If he bought it for $450,000, what is it worth now?

a. $540,000

b. $465,000

c. $501,000

d. $525,000

21. Another name for the government survey method is _____.

a) the rectangular survey system

b) principal surveys

c) base lines survey method

d) principal meridians

22. The Jackson Estate is sold to satisfy a judgment resulting from an $18,000 mechanic's lien for work that began on September 15, 2012, subject to a first mortgage lien of $310,000 recorded November 17, 2011, and to this year's outstanding property taxes of $14,000. If the Estate is sold at the foreclosure sale for $350,000, in what order will the proceeds of the sale be distributed:

a) $310,000 mortgage lien; $18,000 mechanics lien; $14,000 property taxes; $8,000 to the foreclosed landowner

b) $18,000 mechanic's lien; $310,000 mortgage lien; $8,000 foreclosed landowner; $14,000 property taxes

c) $14,000 property taxes; $8,000 foreclosed landowner; $310,000 mortgage lien; $18,000 mechanic's lien

d) $14,000 property taxes; $18,000 mechanic's lien; $310,000 mortgage lien; $8,000 foreclosed landowner

23. Which is subject to property taxes?

a) nonprofit hospital

b) 100-unit apartment complex

c) church

d) golf course operated by the city's parks

24. Kiley, a realtor and interior designer, is more than likely a member of these two associations:

a) NRA and AID

b) NAR and ASID

c) NAR and MAR

d) REA and NRA

25. Public employees use a mill to calculate:

a) hazard insurance premiums

b) mortgage interest

c) trash and sewage rates

d) property tax rates

26. Julie owns five acres of land that she wanted to sell to Kelvin for $800,000. But before she could sell the land to Kelvin she had to first offer it to Angelica, a holder of the right to purchase the land who decided to exercise her right and follow through with the purchase. What right did Angelica exercise?

a) bundle of rights

b) redemption

c) right of first refusal

d) contingency

27. A developer agrees to purchase 50 acres of land from the owner $600,000. The owner has agreed to carry back 20%. If the developer takes out a construction loan with a first lien position, the landowner will have to agree to a _____ agreement.

a) subordination

b) percentage lease

c) conformity

d) deferred transfer

28. A listing agreement is a(n):

a) future delivery purchase

b) interest in severalty

c) estimated amount for which a party should exchange hands

d) contract between a broker and seller

29. Deprecation is accounted for in which approach?

a) market value

b) cost

c) comparative market analysis

d) rent history

30. Although Jesse works as an independent contractor under his broker, the broker is still responsible for all of the following EXCEPT:

a) providing a contract which clearly stipulates that Jesse is responsible for paying quarterly federal income tax payments

b) the ethical and legal behavior of Jesse

c) payment of licensing and professional fees

d) provide an agreement which defines compensation amounts

31. Windstorm insurance is mandated by:

a) federal government

b) state

c) city

d) county

32. The minimum credit score set by FHA in 2010 is:

a) 530

b) 580

c) 620

d) FHA has no minimum credit score

33. A hearing panel found that Mary was in violation of the National Association of Realtors Code of Ethics. In addition to receiving a penalty up to $5,000 what course may she be asked to take?

a) ethics

b) principles of real estate

c) accounting

d) consumer information

34. Which is an example of steering?

a) a lender offers only balloon loans to a certain group of buyers

b) a realtor tells his client to sell his home because one of the neighbors rented his house to a Section 8 tenant

c) an owner decides not to rent his home to a disabled veteran

d) a sales agent begins showing homes to more African Americans in an affluent area because she feels the neighborhood needs to be more integrated

35. Every year Jim and Opal receive an annual allotment of 300 vacation points through their timeshare program. This type of timeshare program is known as:

a) rotation club

b) vacation owner points plan

c) vacation club

d) vacation ownership interest club

36. The following legal description is known as a _____. Lots 3, 4 and 5 in Block 6 of G. Smith's Subdivision, Chesapeake, Virginia.

a) metes and bounds

b) subdivision plat

c) township squares

d) survey system

37. Margaret receives a letter from her homeowners' association that she needs to replace her roof and garage door. She is very upset because she thought these items were covered by the homeowners' association since her unit is attached to other units. What type of unit does Margaret more than likely own?

a) single family residence

b) cooperative

c) townhome

d) condo

38. In Virginia the following two statements: *"The responsibility of the attorney for the mortgagee is to protect the interest of the mortgagee,"* and *"Mortgagors may, at their own expense, engage an attorney of their selection to represent their interests in the transaction,"* must be present on the _____.

a) purchase and sale agreement

b) mortgage application

c) contract offer

d) deed

39. A real estate broker refers his client to US Home Warranty Company and in return they send the broker a $125 referral fee. This is a violation of:

a) the Comprehensive Environmental Response, Compensation, and Liability Act

b) the Real Estate Settlement Procedures Act

c) Truth in Lending

d) HUD-1

40. Which of the following is not a physical characteristic of land?

a. immobility

b. indestructibility

c. non-homogeneity

d. situs

41. In a condominium development, which would be considered a "limited" common element?

a) pool

b) elevator

c) parking slots assigned to occupants

d) limited access gates

42. A signed standard offer-to-purchase form is a binding and enforceable contract to sell real estate under:

a) Virginia case law

b) Virginia general law

c) Virginia county laws

d) none of the above

43. One of the most important deadlines in the contract documents is the:

a) home inspection

b) option period

c) loan commitment

d) none of the above

44. An HO-6 policy is an insurance policy for a(n):

a) PUD

b) SFR

c) mobile home

d) condo

45. The Edwards family is planning on buying a single family home for $319,750. They need to put down 20% in order to buy the home. How much money does the Edwards family need to put down to secure the house?

a. $68,010

b. $63,950

c. $63,600

d. $61,750

46. An appraiser will use the _____ approach to reconcile the values of a three-family rental home.

a) reproduction

b) income

c) cost

d) sales comparison

47. Jane bought her home for $279,000 and now it's worth $333,000. It has _____ in value.

a) appreciated

b) regressed

c) vested

d) diverged

48. Sally received a letter that her home loan with ABC lending was being transferred to Community Bank. This is known as a(n):

a) takeover

b) assumption

c) assignment

d) aggression

49. When a borrower signs a security agreement where he is promising to pay, he is signing a:

a) deed of trust

b) promissory note

c) bill of sale

d) offer contract

50. A disadvantage of a bridge loan is:

a) the buyer does not have to sell their current home before they purchase their next home

b) the lender might not require the buyer to make monthly payments

c) the buyer can immediately put their home on the market

d) buyers may be prequalified based on two mortgages and they might not meet this requirement

51. Henry's title report suggests that the property he's purchasing is free of legal issues and liens, therefore the property has a(n) _____ title.

a) clear

b) cloudy

c) good

d) efficient

52. In a home loan, which is the collateral?

a) the down payment

b) the equity

c) the property

d) the borrower's liquid assets

53. The date an interest rate changes is called the:

a) payment shock

b) balloon maturity date

c) the adjustment date on an adjustable rate loan

d) none of the above

54. Lisa makes an offer on a home and gives her broker a check to let the seller know she is serious. These funds are known as the _____:

a) security deposit

b) earnest money deposit

c) option period deposit

d) down payment

55. Which best describes an easement?

a) When a tenant who is moving out of the storefront he rented takes his cupcake oven

b) A property owner whose land is adjacent to a river, swims and fishes in the river

c) A neighbor accesses his barn by legally crossing part of his neighbor's land

d) The state legally takes back private land to widen the highway

56. A subdivision is:

a) a neighborhood in a community revitalized area

b) a housing development where tracts of land are turned into individual lots

c) when houses in a neighborhood are the same style and color

d) a neighborhood with a homeowners' association board

57. A homebuyer who had limited liquid funds obtained her home through a nonprofit organization; she helped build her home with her own labor and services. What type of contribution did she make?

a) sweat equity

b) equity deposit

c) money

d) labor

58. Ben, who recently lost his job, is considering transferring ownership of his home to his lender as he is having great difficulty making the payments and has been unable to sell it. This is known as:

a) foreclosure

b) deed-in-lieu

c) short sale

d) adverse possession

59. Stephanie and Max, first-time homebuyers in the state are currently living on Stephanie's income as a teacher, but Max will be done with residency in two more years so they know their income will increase dramatically. In light of this, their loan officer has advised them that they could qualify for a little more house if they took out a loan that increased by no more than 7.5% per year over the next five years. What type of loan are they being offered?

a) four-step mortgage

b) fixed rate

c) two-to-one buy down

d) graduated payment

60. **According to their lender, a couple must contribute $71,700 in the form of a cashier's check toward the purchase of the $478,000 home they would like to purchase. This amount is known as the:**

a) earnest money deposit

b) junior mortgage

c) down payment

d) contingency fee

61. **For government loans, which statement is true?**

a) They are insured by FHA.

b) They are guaranteed by RHS.

c) They are guaranteed by VA.

d) All of the above.

62. **Heather conveyed her interest in a property to her brother, Barry's friend, Mike's parents, Mr. and Mrs. Olsen. Who is the grantee?**

a) Mike

b) Mr. and Mrs. Olsen

c) Heather

d) Barry

63. **Katy and Mickey's home was completely destroyed during the hurricane. When they returned to check the damage, they found their basement completely flooded and everything destroyed as the water level reached up to the second floor. Which insurance will more than likely cover the bulk of the damages?**

a) hurricane

b) windstorm

c) flood

d) hazard

64. Which is NOT a liquid asset?

a) money in savings account

b) 401(k)

c) parcel of land

d) stocks

65. A homebuyer used a mortgage broker with Finance World to get her home loan. She used the payment coupon provided to her mail her first payment to Finance World. Before her second payment was due, she received a letter stating that her loan was being assigned to the Bank of the United States and that the investor Duchess Bank had remained the same. Which is her current lender?

a) Finance World

b) Duchess Bank

c) Bank of the United States

d) Mortgage broker

66. If Justine has power of attorney, she has been granted?

a) limited or full authority to make decisions on behalf of someone else

b) an opportunity to represent someone in court

c) entrance to law school

d) full power to make medical decisions on behalf of someone else

67. The principal is:

a) that part of the mortgage payment that reduces the unpaid balance

b) the amount borrowed

c) a and b

d) neither a nor b

68. Which best describes an encroachment?

a) You legally drive across part of your neighbor's property to access your property.

b) You continuously use your neighbor's driveway for years and he doesn't stop you.

c) You add a non-legal second level to your home which completely blocks your neighbors view to the sea.

d) You allow your horses to drink out of the river which is adjacent to your land.

69. Two sons are joint tenants in a property left to them by their parents. Son A has one child and Son B has four children. In the event Son B dies, who does the property go to?

a) the property is split equally among the five grandchildren

b) the property goes to Son A and his child

c) the property goes to Son B's children

d) the property goes to Son A only

70. Ansley wants to see a visual representation of when her mortgage will be paid off as well as how much money she will be paying in interest each year. This is known as a(n):

a) loan payment schedule

b) amortization schedule

c) interest rate table

d) rate sheet

71. A biweekly payment is one in which:

a) the homeowner will make her mortgage payment every two weeks

b) the homeowner will make her mortgage payment every other month

c) the homeowner will make a payment one time every month, but on the last month of the year two payments will be made

d) the homeowner will make half of her mortgage payment every two weeks

72. Kelly is told that her ARM loan has an initial interest rate of 5.5% and that as the rate adjusts it can never go above 9%. Nine percent is the _____ for her loan.

a) buy-down

b) APR

c) cap

d) *ad valorem*

73. Virginia is a _____ settlement state.

a) wet

b) dry

c) contingency

d) covenant

74. Henry sells his home to his friend Reese; then Henry gets a letter from his lender demanding full payment. The mortgage included a _____.

a) acceleration clause

b) deed restriction

c) due-on-sale clause

d) covenant of seisin

75. Murray had to go to court to get his property back from his nephew because when he granted him the property he told him that he could not sell alcohol on the premises. What type of estate was this?

a) homestead

b) ordinary with remainder or reversion

c) determinable fee estate

d) fee simple subject to a condition subsequent with right of reentry

76. Which provides the best range of property values on a particular property?

a) competitive market analysis

 b) broker price opinions

c) appraisal

d) income approach

77. Jenn and Mike finally found the home of their dreams within their budget of $385,000. They had already been pre-approved for a loan based on 75% loan-to-value. If the sales price

is $380,000 but the appraisal came in at $365,500, what is the max loan the lender will give them for this home?

a) $288,750

b) $380,000

c) $285,000

d) $274,125

78. The Commonwealth of Virginia generates revenue from the sale of real estate through:

a) commissions

b) transfer tax

c) down payments

d) broker and salesperson license fees

79. Jerry, an attorney whose principal residence is in Maine, has decided to get his Virginia broker's license. What must he do to get the license?

a) take 60 classroom hours and pass the real estate exam

b) make Virginia his principal residence

c) review and follow the guidelines for Maine's reciprocity agreement with Virginia

d) pass the real estate exam only

80. Wilford transfers one of his small rental units to his son for $1.00. What will the transfer tax charge be?

a) $0

b) $1,000

c) $4.45

d) $456

81. Martha pays her taxes and insurance every month along with her mortgage payment. This is known as a(n) _____ mortgage.

a) equity

b) budget

c) escrow

d) negative amortization

82. A very famous couple chooses a city apartment near all of the amenities they enjoy so they don't have to travel too far out and risk being noticed. Their agent notifies them they did not receive approval because the condo association board believes they will disrupt the peace and quiet currently enjoyed by the residents. Which best describes this scenario?

a) The condo association can vote in or out whoever they feel is a good match (or not) for the condo development.

b) The Board is violating the Civil Rights Act of 1866.

c) Celebrities are a protected class and cannot be discriminated against.

d) Coops can deny or approve the sale of shares of stock if they feel someone may jeopardize the quiet enjoyment the residents currently enjoy.

83. The realtor tells a couple that because of regression, they may have to list their home at a different price than anticipated. Which best describes what is happening?

a) the neighboring homes haven't been updated and modernized as much as the subject property

b) the home has an outdated floor plan

c) the home is in disrepair

d) a school was recently built around the corner

84. **When Broker Jamie takes his client's earnest money deposit and puts it in his personal account to tide him over until his next commission check comes, which fiduciary duty is he not living up to?**

a) dedication

b) accounting

c) obedience

d) confidentiality

85. **The Homestead Act does NOT protect you from which of the following:**

a) credit cards

b) the proceeds from the sale of your home

c) a Medicaid lien from a nursing home stay

d) the proceeds from your insurance claim if your home was damaged by fire

86. **The following is which type of description commonly used in Virginia legal descriptions: North 34 degrees East 200 feet to point.**

a) reference

b) bounded

c) strip

d) metes

87. **Katy has a voluntary lien on her home. Which represents a voluntary lien?**

a) mortgage

b) property tax

c) federal IRS

d) mechanic's lien

88. Samantha's condominium unit which recently appraised at $413,000, was recently damaged in a storm. If it was currently assessed at $405,000, what is the minimum amount covered by her HO-6 policy?

a) $81,000

b) $82,600

c) $80,000

d) $84,000

89. A broker is listing a home where he knows a homicide was committed. Under the Uniform Deceptive Trade Practices Act:

a) the broker has a fiduciary duty to disclose this to potential buyers

b) the broker must disclose the sequence of events related to the homicide

c) the broker cannot hold any open houses

d) the broker has no legal duty to inform buyers

90. Jane has a document which states she has legal rights of ownership for 1324 Elm St, Any City, Virginia 45678. This document is known as:

a) affidavit

b) quitclaim deed

c) title

d) trustee deed

91. Gerard has a 30-year loan where his interest rate is 5% for five years, then increases to 6% for the life of the loan. What type of mortgage does he have?

a) fixed rate mortgage

b) modification

c) two-step mortgage

d) fully amortized

92. The buyers purchasing Geoff's vacation home love his furnishings so much they want to buy all of them. What contract should he use in this type of sale?

a) bill of sale

b) grant deed

c) purchase and sale agreement

d) quitclaim deed

93. Mr. Jethendrux has appointed an executrix to handle his final affairs. Which person could this have been?

a) Kathryn

b) James

c) both a and b

d) neither a nor b

94. Which is the best description of a real estate agent?

a) Anyone, licensed or not, who conducts and/or negotiates the sale of real estate

b) The owner and manager of a real estate firm

c) A person who sells both home warranties and property

d) A person who is licensed who conducts and negotiates the sale of real estate

95. Ricky's friend Esther is leaving the country. She has a great loan with a 3.5% interest rate and a remaining term of 20 years. Because Ricky would like to take over this loan, he sends her lender all of his income and asset documents. Ricky is trying to get a(n) _____.

a) primary mortgage

b) assumption

c) refinance

d) equity loan

96. A legal document which conveys title to a property is known as a:

a) deed

b) preliminary title report

c) purchase and sale agreement

d) promissory note

97. Which is the most common type of bankruptcy?

a) Chapter 13

b) Chapter 7 no assets

c) Chapter 13 no assets

d) Chapter 7

98. Someone's credit history report is prepared by a _____.

a) mortgage broker

b) underwriter

c) credit bureau

d) notary public

99. Paula made her mortgage payment 30 days past its due date. Her mortgage is now in:

a) arrears

b) default

c) foreclosure

d) bankruptcy

100. What is the age an appraiser uses to describe a property's physical condition?

a) effective age

b) longevity

c) year built

d) average age

Real Estate Sales Exam III Answers

1. d. $428. In Virginia, the seller pays a grantor tax of $0.50 per $500.

2. a. In Virginia, a first-time salesperson licensee must complete 30 hours of continuing education in the first two years.

3. a. Virginia has reciprocity agreements with 49 states.

4. b. As long as they apply to the correct municipality and get approved, the blind, elderly, veterans, surviving spouses, and children are exempt from property taxes.

5. c. A management agreement is between the owner of income property and the property manager which details the scope of work expected by the property manager.

6. a. The Equal Credit Opportunity Act protects against discrimination in lending.

7. c. They are doing the mortgaging, so they are the mortgagor.

8. d. Coops are transferred as shares of stock in which there is no recording and because of this, individual property taxes are not created for the unit, but rather the coop or corporation pays a property tax bill for the development and passes along each member's portion to be paid through their monthly maintenance fee.

9. b. The cut trees are moveable so they are personal property.

10. c. A vendee is also known as the purchaser.

11. c. In order to file for adverse possession, you must prove you have continuously used the property for 15 years, without any warning from the owner.

12. d. Both parties are free to renegotiate.

13. c. Equity is the difference between the value and the liens.

14. b. A contingency clause is when a certain act must be accomplished within a given amount of time.

15. a. Of the six agent responsibilities, obedience, loyalty, disclosure, confidentiality, accounting and reasonable care, the agent showed loyalty to her clients by putting their interest above her own.

16. c. "Taking" is when the municipality takes action against a property owner and through the court land process attempts to gain ownership of the property.

17. d. FHA insures the lender against borrower default.

18. a. With a voidable contract the law gives one party an option whether or not to proceed with the agreement.

19. b. Real property refers to the land and things or items that are permanently attached to it, e.g. plant life, houses, etc. Any fixed item that can cause damage to the property when it is moved is real property. Personal property refers to property that is moveable such as furniture, and will not cause any damage to the property.

20. a. $450,000 X .02= $9000 increased value each year. Take increased value and multiply it by the number of years the property has been owned. $9,000 X 10= $90,000. Add the total increased value to sell price. $450,000 + $90,000 = $540,000.

21. a. The rectangular survey system.

22. d. In Virginia, order of payment is municipal lien, federal tax lien, state tax lien, mechanic's lien, and all other liens on order of recording, seller.

23. b. Nonprofits are exempt from paying property taxes.

24. b. Realtors are member of the National Association of Realtors and many interior designers are members of the American Society of Interior Designers.

25. d. One mill is equal to one tenth of one penny or one 1/1000th of a dollar and mills are often used when expressing property tax rates.

26. c. In a right of first refusal the owner gives the holder of the right an opportunity to enter into a transaction with the owner before the owner can enter into a transaction with another party.

27. a. Subordination agreements change the priority of a mortgage or lien.

28. d. Listing agreement is a contract between a broker and seller.

29. b. Depreciation is estimated in the cost approach.

30. c. The contract must stipulate that the agent is responsible for paying their own licensing and professional fees.

31. c. Windstorm insurance is governed by the state.

32. b. The minimum credit score set by FHA in 2010 is 580.

33. a. She may be asked to take an ethics course through the association.

34. d. Steering is the illegal practice of directing potential homebuyers away from or to particular areas.

35. c. Vacation clubs are newer timeshare programs which give members an annual allotment of points.

36. b. The subdivision plat method uses descriptions of lots and block numbers.

37. c. With a townhome purchase, the buyer purchases the individual unit and the ground below it. In addition, each unit generally has its own roof and home amenities like garages.

38. b. The wording must appear on the mortgage application.

39. b. RESPA prohibits kickbacks.

40. d. Situs is an economic characteristic of land, not a physical characteristic of land.

41. c. Parking spaces assigned to occupants are "limited" to that occupant.

42. a. Under Virginia case law a signed standard offer-to-purchase form is a binding and enforceable contract to sell real estate even if the offer is subject to a purchase and sale agreement.

43. c. The loan commitment deadline is one of the most important deadlines.

44. d. An HO-6 policy, much like a hazard insurance policy for a home, is now required for condominiums by FNMA and FHA.

45. b. Find the answer by taking the cost of the home $319,750 and multiplying it by 20% or .20.

46. b. The income approach is used to estimate the value of income-producing properties.

47. a. When a home appreciates, it increases in value.

48. c. Assignment is when mortgage ownership is transferred from one company to another.

49. b. A note is a promise to pay.

50. d. Often, bridge loan lenders will prequalify buyers for two home loans.

51. a. Clear title is free of liens and legal questions.

52. c. Because the borrower can lose the property due to non-payment, the property itself is the collateral.

53. c. The adjustment date on an adjustable rate loan is the date an interest rate changes

54. b. The earnest money deposit lets the seller know the buyer is serious.

55. c. An easement occurs when someone other than the owner has right of way legal access

56. b. Developers divide up tracts of land to create individual lots

57. a. When labor or services are provided in lieu of cash, this is known as sweat equity.

58. b. Deed-in-lieu is when the homeowner voluntarily transfers the title to the lender in exchange for release of lien and payment.

59. d. A graduated payment mortgage is one in which the payment can increase by 7.5% per year over a period of time usually 5 years and then remains the same for the duration of the loan.

60. c. The down payment is generally made in the form of a cashier's check and is the initial amount that the buyer contributes upfront towards the total amount due.

61. d. Government loans are guaranteed by the Veterans Administration and Rural Housing and insured by FHA.

62. b. The person(s) who receive title to a property is/are the grantee.

63. c. Because the home was damaged by the excessive water level and experienced significant flooding, the flood insurance will cover the damages.

64. c. A liquid asset is one that can be easily converted to cash.

65. b. The lender is the actual financial institution that lent the money.

66. a. Power of attorney grants an individual full or limited authority on behalf of someone else.

67. c. The principal is the amount of money borrowed and it also refers to that part of the mortgage payment that reduces the unpaid balance.

68. c. An encroachment is an illegal improvement which intrudes on another's property.

69. d. Joint tenancy has right of survivorship; the survivor will now receive the deceased's portion of the property.

70. b. An amortization schedule is a table that shows how much principal will be applied out of each mortgage payment. It also shows the yearly balance as it decreases until it reaches zero.

71. d. With a bi-weekly mortgage payment the homeowner pays half the monthly mortgage payment every two weeks; by the end of the year they will have made the equivalent of 13 payments.

72. c. The limit on ARM loans.

73. a. Virginia is a wet settlement state. Wet settlement is when funding occurs at closing.

74. c. A due-on-sale clause allows the lender to demand full repayment if the borrower sells the property that serves as security for the loan.

75. d. A fee simple subject to a condition subsequent with right of reentry is where the grantor can go to court to get title back to his property if the grantee does not comply with the grantor's condition of ownership.

76. a. The competitive market analysis helps the licensed agent/broker to identify a range of values in a given area.

77. d. The lender will lend based on the appraised value which is $365,500. 75% of $365,500 = $274,125.

78. b. Virginia generates revenue from the sale of real estate through transfer taxes.

79. c. Virginia has reciprocity with all other US states for real estate licenses. He should look at the specific guidelines for his home state's reciprocity agreement with Virginia.

80. a. When the transfer is for less than $100, the Bureau of Land Records will not charge transfer tax.

81. b. A budget mortgage is when the lender pulls funds from the borrower's monthly payment and sets it aside in an escrow account in order to make yearly tax and insurance payments.

82. d. While they are bound by fair housing laws and cannot discriminate based on age, gender, ethnicity/race and religion, coops do have more control than condo associations since they transfer share of stock as opposed to real property.

83. a. In this case regression describes the fact that improvements have been made to the subject property that are much greater than the neighboring homes.

84. b. The fiduciary duty of accounting states that the agent cannot commingle funds.

85. c. A Medicaid lien is a government lien and they are exempt.

86. d. Metes description gives both a bearing and a distance.

87. a. A voluntary lien is created by the lienee's action.

88. b. The HO-6 policy must provide for a minimum of 20% of the appraised value.

89. d. According to the Uniform Deceptive Trade Practices Act, "The fact or suspicion that real property may be or is psychologically impacted shall not be deemed to be a material fact required to be disclosed in a real estate transaction."

90. c. Title is a legal document evidencing a person's right or ownership to real property.

91. c. A two-step mortgage generally starts out at a set interest rate then increases after 5 or 7 years to a higher set rate for the duration of the loan.

92. a. A bill of sale is used in transferring personal property.

93. d. An executrix is a female appointed to administer a will.

94. d. A real estate agent is a licensed person who conducts and negotiates the sale of real estate.

95. b. An assumption is when a buyer takes over the seller's mortgage.

96. a. A deed is a legal document which conveys title to property.

97. b. A "Chapter 7 no asset" is when the filer has no assets to pay the creditors.

98. c. A credit bureau is a third party company that prepares a summary report of an individual's credit history.

99. b. Generally, payments 30 days behind on first trust deeds are said to be in default.

100. a. The effective age is a term the appraiser uses to describe a building's physical condition.

Real Estate Sales Exam IV

1. The sum of all of Mr. Slayer's personal property and real estate at the time of his death is known as his:

a) probate

b) escheat

c) estate

d) will

2. Melody's dad, a cabinet maker, built her a beautiful entertainment unit that he securely attached to her wall five years ago. Now that she's married and she and her husband want to grow their family they have decided to move. The unit will have to remain in the home because it is a(n):

a) easement

b) trade fixture

c) appurtenance

d) fixture

3. A homeowner's insurance policy:

a) is a warranty service contract that covers repair and replacement of home appliances

b) combines hazard insurance and personal liability insurance

c) is hazard insurance

d) all of the above

4. A servicer:

a) lends money to purchase a home

b) collects mortgage payments from borrowers

c) conducts title searches

d) insures the loan in case of borrower default

5. A three-family home in Virginia is:

a) a dwelling with one deed that is for three families

b) a commercial property

c) not legal in Virginia

d) a dwelling with three different deeds that is for three families

6. Three homeowners live adjacent to a body of water, but their water use rights are based on when they first used or applied for use. This is known as:

a) riparian rights

b) littoral rights

c) the doctrine of prior appropriation

d) the doctrine of adverse possession

7. A tenancy that is NOT put in place by operation of law but by the parties expressed intent is:

a) tenancy at will

b) tenancy by the entirety

c) community property

d) tenancy in common

8. All are "improvements" except:

a) sidewalk

b) street light

c) pizza oven

d) paved road

9. Which is NOT a physical characteristic of land?

a) scarcity

b) non-homogeneity

c) immobility

d) indestructibility

10. Over several years, the Parsons' land ownership has increased by means of:

a) regression

b) accretion

c) diversion

d) avulsion

11. David allows Mike to store his pickup truck in his driveway for several weeks free of charge. David gave Mike a(n) _____.

a) acknowledgment

b) tenancy right

c) license

d) easement by prescription

12. Marty receives a notice for specific performance of a real estate contract, which is asking for:

a) an earnest money deposit

b) conveyance of the property

c) a new contract

d) a deficiency judgment

13. Which is NOT an acceptable means by which a contract can be terminated?

a) sellers decide to get a divorce during transaction

b) destruction of premises

c) mutual agreement of the parties to cancel

d) impossibility of performance

14. Timothy is out of town when his broker tries to inform him that she has a buyer for his home who has made a full price bid and given her (the broker) the $3,000 earnest money deposit. What does the broker have at this point?

a) an implied contract

b) an executed purchase and sale agreement

c) a voidable contract

d) an offer

15. Patricia, who fell behind on her mortgage payments, requested assistance from her lender. Her lender helped her by replacing her old mortgage with a new one in which they lowered her interest rate and extended her term. What best describes what happened?

a) refinancing

b) novation

c) accelerating

d) none of the above

16. Which of the following statements is TRUE of a listing contract?

a) It obligates the broker to convince the seller to convey the property to the first person to make an offer.

b) It maintains that the broker act as a non-agent with a seller.

c) It is an employment contract between the broker and the principal.

d) It is an agreement that lasts indefinitely.

17. Which statement represents what an exclusive-agency listing and an exclusive-right-to-sell listing have in common?

a) Both provide for only one broker to represent the seller.

b) Both are net listings.

c) With both, the seller only allows only one salesperson to show his property.

d) With both, the seller can sell the property without paying a commission.

18. Margaret's broker listed and advertised her property, to find Nathan, a ready, willing and able buyer. After reviewing the offer and sleeping on it, Margaret decided to reject the offer, telling her agent she had remorse and no longer wished to sell her home. In this case Margaret:

a) will have to pay the buyers for any damages

b) must sell the property

c) owes her broker the commission

d) is within her rights to change her mind

19. Highest and best use is:

a) the effective age of a property

b) what results in its "highest value"

c) the most marketable value

d) the book value

20. All are significant factors in comparing property with the sales comparison approach EXCEPT:

a) original purchase price

b) financing terms

c) physical appearance and condition

d) sale date

21. PITI stands for:

a) payment, insurance, taxes and investment

b) principal, insurance, tariff, interest

c) payment, interest, taxes, insurance

d) principal, interest, taxes and insurance

22. Samantha has a 15-year loan at 4.5% interest rate for 15 years. This is a:

a) conventional fixed rate loan

b) fixed rate loan

c) variable loan

d) pay option arm loan

23. You should use which formula to calculate the gross income multiplier (GIM):

a) GIM = annual gross income/sales price

b) GIM = rate x value

c) GIM = sales price/annual gross income

d) GIM = value/rate

24. When a property is pledged for a loan without giving up possession, this is known as:

a) substitution

b) acceleration

c) hypothecation

d) alienation

25. Greg is someone who has received training, education and is experienced in estimating real property value. His job title is a(n):

a) loan processor

b) mortgage banker

c) underwriter

d) appraiser

26. Another name for homeowners' association dues is:

a) community property fees

b) common area assessments

c) common law dues

d) apportionments

27. A(n) _____ is when a tenant is lawfully expelled from the property.

a) aversion

b) eviction

c) conviction

d) avulsion

28. Which of these does NOT describe a duty of a recorder?

a) a public official who maintains public real estate records

b) county clerk

c) transcribes real estate transaction

d) collects fees for documents filed

29. Hank and Cheri use a 1003 to:

a) apply for a mortgage loan

b) write out a land contract

c) list a property for sale

d) make an offer on a home

30. Once the appraisal was completed, Jet's lender received a CRV or Certificate of Reasonable Value. What type of loan is he getting?

a) Fannie Mae

b) FHA

c) RHS

d) VA

31. _____ and _____ are Government Sponsored Entities.

a) FHA and VA

b) Ginnie Mae and Freddie Mac

c) Fannie Mae and Freddie Mac

d) RHS and Agricultural loans

32. According to Regulation Z, Jasmine has _____ to rescind the transaction.

a) 5 days

b) 3 days

c) 4 days

d) 1 day

33. An employer-sponsored tax-deferred retirement plan that homebuyers can borrower against is a:

a) 401(k)

b) 203(k)

c) 403(b)

d) a and c

34. Jumbo loans exceed _____.

a) $417,000

b) $650,000

c) $471,000

d) $617,000

35. The Fair and Accurate Credit Transactions Act of 2003 (FACTA) deals with:

a) mortgage fraud

b) commingling of funds

c) prepayment penalties

d) identity theft

36. Which statement about mortgage insurance is NOT true?

a) is also known as private mortgage insurance

b) covers the lender when a homeowner defaults

c) is required when the borrower's down payment is 20% or more

d) is included in the mortgage payment

37. The Barksdale family just learned that the city is planning to build a small commuter airport near their family farm in which the home will sit below the flight path. They were hoping to sell the farm in a year but now fear that their values may be decreased due to:

a) functional obsolescence

b) functional regression

c) economic obsolescence

d) economic regression

38. Two years ago, 17-year-old Jonathan inherited five two family homes from his late father. Now two years later, Jonathan has decided to sell one of them. If he conveys his interest in the property to a purchaser by signing a deed, the contract will be:

a) valid

b) void

c) voidable

d) invalid

39. Valid exclusive listings must include:

a) an expiration date

b) a forfeiture clause

c) an automatic renewal clause

d) must allow the listing broker to appoint subagents

40. Meredith wanted Haley to know that her signature was genuine as she was signing a deed transferring ownership of her property to Haley. The declaration that Meredith made before a notary was a(n):

a) sheriff's deed

b) acknowledgment

c) promissory note

d) affidavit

41. Title to real estate can be transferred by involuntary alienation by all of the following except:

a) escheat

b) erosion

c) seisin

d) eminent domain

42. During her closing, Hillary reviewed a legal document which requires that she repay her mortgage loan during a given period of time based on a stated interest rate. This document is known as a:

a) mortgage

b) deed of trust

c) lien

d) note

43. Zachary, whose home is set to close in two weeks, gets a call from his builder saying that his new home won't be ready for another three weeks. Zachary's realtor works out a deal where he can remain in the home a week after closing. This is known as a:

a) leasehold

b) leaseback

c) lease at will

d) lease purchase

44. A trustee is:

a) a fiduciary who controls property for the benefit of another person

b) always the executor of the estate

c) a trustworthy individual

d) an attorney

45. The best type of estate to inherit is:

a) a leasehold estate

b) a life estate

c) a fee simple estate

d) a general estate

46. The time and date a document was recorded establish:

a) chain of title

b) subrogation

c) escrow

d) priority

47. Rich sells a parcel of land to Tom. Tom quickly records the deed. If Rich tries to sell the same parcel to Kevin, which of the following statements is TRUE?

a) Tom will have to bring a quitclaim deed to court, since Rich is trying to sell the same property.

b) Kevin has been given constructive notice of the prior sale because Tom quickly recorded the deed.

c) Kevin was mailed the actual notice of the prior sale since Tom recorded the deed.

d) none of the above

48. The acquisition of real estate through the payment of money is:

a) a sales transaction

b) called a truth in lending transaction

c) a purchase money transaction

d) a deed-in-lieu

49. A property sales price is a:

a) debit to the buyer and a credit to the seller

b) credit to the buyer only

c) debit to the seller and credit to the buyer

d) credit to the seller only

50. Wilma collected a security deposit from each of her tenants when they signed their lease agreements. Now that she is selling her property, who should be credit the security deposits?

a) Wilma

b) buyer

c) tenants

d) lender

51. Because Jimmy has the right to control his property, he has a right to do all of the following except:

a) refuse to host a neighborhood block meeting at his home

b) turn away the meter reader from the local utility company

c) put a sign in his front yard that says "no soliciting"

d) host a family barbeque

52. Two properties A and B are separated by a private road. Landowner A owns the road but Landowner B has unrestricted access to the road, as he needs to use the road to reach the highway. What type of access does Landowner B have?

a) an easement by necessity

b) an encroachment

c) an easement

d) an assessment

53. Mena was so excited as she was purchasing her first home and everything, so far, had gone smoothly. The home inspection came back with minimal issues and her loan was fully approved. But two days before her closing date, the home caught on fire and was totally destroyed. Who will more than likely bear the loss?

a) Mena

b) the seller's lender

c) the seller

d) the buyer's lender

54. Contracts for the sale of real property, under the statute of frauds, must be:

a) in writing to be enforceable

b) on purchase and sale agreement forms

c) started by a licensed agent

d) executed right away

55. The Martins enter into a sales contract with the Haggardy family in which they will pay the Haggardy family $1,500 per month for their family farm. The Martins will pay all insurance premiums, property taxes, and any maintenance and repair costs, but the Haggardys will maintain title to the property for 20 years. What type of contract do the families have?

a) lease with option to buy

b) contract for deed

c) contract at will

d) mortgage contract

56. Harry lists his home with Broker Bill. He tells Broker Bill that as long as he receives net proceeds of $203,000 from the sale of his home, Broker Bill can keep the difference as commission. This type of listing is known as:

a) an exclusive-agency listing

b) an open listing

c) an exclusive-right-to-sell listing

d) net listing

57. The original capital outlay for labor, materials, land and profit is known as:

a) the market value

b) the market price

c) the mortgage value

d) the cost

58. Kenny, a single man, died and left all of his real estate to his niece, 23-year-old Ashley in a will. Title passes to Ashley at what point?

a) when she executes a new deed to all of the properties

b) after she pays all of the property taxes

c) immediately upon Kenny's death

d) once she receives a title report that the properties are free and clear

59. How does a condominium differ from a planned unit development (PUD)?

a) a condominium usually has a pool and gym

b) in a PUD, an owner owns the building or unit they live in

c) a PUD has more units

d) all of above are true

60. A rate and term refinance:

a) is also known as a no cash-out refinance

b) generally covers the previous balance plus the costs associated with obtaining the new mortgage

c) puts cash in the borrower's hands

d) both a and b

61. Existing mortgages are usually bought as a "pool" on the _____.

a) primary market

b) secondary market

c) government market

d) black market

62. Liens and encumbrances shown on the title commitment, other than those listed in the contract, must be removed so that the title can be conveyed free and clear. It is the _____ responsibility to remove these.

a) seller's

b) buyer's

c) lender's

d) title company's

63. The principal amount of the buyer's new mortgage is a:

a) debit to the real estate company

b) credit to the real estate company

c) credit to the buyer

d) debit to the seller

64. Jay's lender would like to ensure that he is paying a fair price for the home he is purchasing. In order to determine this, the lender will order a(n):

a) appraisal

b) broker price opinion

c) comparative market analysis

d) chain of title

65. For tax purposes, a(n) _____ establishes the value of a property.

a) broker

b) recorder

c) appraiser

d) assessor

66. Which tenancy automatically renews itself at each expiration?

a) tenancy at sufferance

b) tenancy for years

c) tenancy from month to month

d) tenancy at will

67. A valid lease has all of the requirements EXCEPT:

a) valuable consideration

b) offer and acceptance

c) capacity to contract

d) county clerk recording

68. Money set aside for the replacement of common property in a condominium or cooperative project is called:

a) replacement reserve fund

b) savings fund

c) capital improvements fund

d) contingency fund

69. Judith had to replace her boiler. This type of repair is classified as which type of maintenance?

a) construction

b) corrective

c) preventive

d) routine

70. Which does NOT affect zoning?

a) The principle of conformity enhances value.

b) The city requests that new building conform to specific types of architecture.

c) Values have remained the same because owners have the freedom to develop land as they please.

d) A new city ordinance mandates that the street floor of an office building be used for delis and cafes.

71. Happy Family Realty received a *lis pendens* for their recent listing located at 7892 Oak Street. They now have:

a) a notice of special assessment

b) a notice that legal action has been filed which could affect the title to the property

c) a loan commitment letter

d) a home inspection report

72. New agent Barbara was so excited to close her first client that she gave her friend Nicholas $200 for referring the client to her. What Barbara did was:

a) give Nicholas what is considered a kickback and is illegal under RESPA

b) legal as it's the cost of doing business

c) as long as Barbara had her attorney draw up an agreement between her and Nicholas, this was legal

d) illegal because she should have given the money to her broker

73. Which is an example of a unilateral contract?

a) a real estate sales contract

b) an agreement which states that you will provide sweat equity as your contribution in having your home built.

c) a contract between a broker and his agent

d) The sales manager says he will offer a 20% bonus if you sell $3.5 million in real estate.

74. The Gramm-Leach Bliley Act (GLBA) requires that companies give consumers privacy notices. Which jurisdiction does this fall under?

a) The Equal Credit Opportunity Act

b) Community Reinvestment Act

c) The Federal Trade Commission

d) The Sherman Antitrust Law

75. All are loan payment plans EXCEPT:

a) 30-year-fixed loan at 5.5% interest rate

b) two-to-one buy down

c) reverse mortgage

d) graduated payment mortgage

76. A primary mortgage loan is funded by:

a) a mortgage banker

b) a mortgage broker

c) both a and b

d) neither a nor b

77. What should an owner of an apartment complex do if he has determined that his vacancy rate is less than 4%?

a) Nothing

b) He should lower his advertising budget.

c) He should make property improvements.

d) He should survey the rental market to determine whether he can raise his rents.

78. Jacob and Leslie have a beautiful 2,700 square foot home just outside the city, but most of the other homes are about 1,800 square feet. Their home value has decreased because of what appraisal principle?

a) regression

b) assemblage

c) diminishing and increasing returns

d) contribution and conformity

79. Under FIRREA appraisers need to be licensed by the _____ in order to appraise real property valued over $1,000,000 in federally related transactions.

a) state

b) federal government

c) county

d) bank

80. The house on Elm Drive is for sale because last year someone committed suicide in the home. In Virginia, a listing broker:

a) must tell the buyer

b) must tell the buyer's agent

c) must tell the lender

d) does not have to disclose this information according to Virginia general law.

81. A buyer's agent should NOT disclose which of the following to the seller?

a) the relationship between the buyer and the agent

b) agent compensation that will be paid from the broker's commission

c) that the agent may benefit from referring the parties to a subsidiary of the broker's firm

d) that the buyer is anxious to find a place to live

82. The art of weighing the findings and analyzing from three approaches to value is known as:

a) substitution

b) reconciliation

c) assumption

d) capitalization

83. A prospective buyer is attracted to a property that has a negative cash flow. The following is very likely to be TRUE?

a) the depreciable base is large

b) there is no deferred maintenance

c) there is a substantial increase in property value

d) the new buyer will have to make a huge down payment

84. What provision can stop Cary from losing her home to foreclosure if she files for Chapter 13 bankruptcy?

a) automatic stay provision

b) automatic stop provision

c) repayment provision

d) payment restructure provision

85. Lisa is frustrated with her homeowners' association as they have neglected to fix the walkway where her mother fell. She should:

a) stop paying her HOA dues

b) continue to pay her HOA dues because in Virginia HOA dues take precedence over all other liens

c) place the money she would normally pay for her dues in an escrow account until the repairs are made

d) fix the walkway with the money she would normally pay her HOA dues and send the HOA a bill

86. If you bought your home 20 years ago for $80,000 and now the value is $225,000, at what percent did the house appreciate each year?

a. 23%

b. 7%

c. 12%

d. 9%

87. Raymond's commitment letter which has not expired states his interest rate will be 4.75%. But now his lender tells him that he forgot to lock that rate in and his new rate will be 5.25%. If Raymond has met all of the lender requirements, which is true?

a) He will have to pay the new rate of 5.25%.

b) The lender will be reprimanded.

c) Under Virginia law the commitment letter may be a binding agreement.

d) Raymond will have to pay the discount points to get the 4.75% rate.

88. In some states the sellers must sign the seller's disclosure. In Virginia:

a) sellers are not required to sign the disclosure

b) sellers must disclose ALL defects

c) sellers are required to sign the disclosure

d) sellers do not have to disclose a known leak

89. The Virginia Circuit Breaker Tax Credit deals with:

a) electrical wiring in the home

b) property tax credits

c) personal property tax credits

d) riparian rights

90. Which situation below deals with the Spite Fence Law?

a) A neighbor puts up a 7-foot-tall fence tall unattractive fence to get back at his neighbor.

b) A neighbor puts up a 5-foot-tall fence to keep his small dog in his yard.

c) A neighbor puts up a 6-foot-tall fence for privacy as he has small children who play in the back yard.

d) A neighbor puts up a 5-foot-tall fence on part of his neighbor's property.

91. In Virginia, "an ownership that arises between a husband and wife when a single instrument transfers property to both of them and says nothing about the type of ownership" is:

a) joint tenancy

b) tenancy in common

c) tenancy of sufferance

d) tenancy by the entirety

92. All are public records that may not be found through a title search EXCEPT:

a) mistakes in recording legal documents

b) unpaid liens

c) forged deed

d) fraud

93. Mr. and Mrs. Banks have made their last mortgage payment as they have paid off their home loan. They are now ready to record their discharge. In Virginia, how much should they expect to pay for this?

a) $75.00

b) $125.00

c) $50.00

d) $35.00

94. Which is NOT a condition that makes a Virginia purchase offer conditional?

a) home inspection

b) financing contingency

c) earnest money deposit

d) review of the purchase and sale agreement by an attorney

95. Ownership of a property by one person is known as:

a) remainder interest

b) entirety

c) severalty

d) reversionary interest

96. The words of conveyance in a deed are in the:

a) purchase clause

b) selling clause

c) granting clause

d) heading

97. Which of the following properties will have the highest capitalization rate?

a) a modernized school

b) an SFR

c) a convenience store

d) a small shopping center with limited traffic access

98. Open listings are also known as:

a) multiple listings

b) nonexclusive agreements

c) exclusive rights to sell

d) net listings

99. Gilbert defaulted on his loan and the lender foreclosed. Which clause requires the lender to look only to the property for satisfaction of debt?

a) exculpatory clause

b) deficiency judgment

c) acceleration clause

d) defeasance clause

100. Grantees are protected by express covenants found in the:

a) bill of sale deed

b) quit claim deed

c) general warranty deed

d) sheriff's deed

Real Estate Sales Exam IV Answers

1. c. The sum total of an individual's personal and real property at the time of death

2. d. A fixture is personal property that is attached to the real property.

3. b. A homeowner's insurance policy combines hazard insurance and personal liability insurance.

4. b. A servicer collects mortgage payments from a borrower.

5. a. A three-family home is a dwelling for three families and ownership is evidence by one deed.

6. c. The doctrine of prior appropriation is generally in areas of water scarcity. Water rights are assigned priority based on when the right was either first used or applied for.

7. b. Tenancy by the entirety is a tenancy a husband and wife can choose that is typically not recognized in community property states.

8. c. A trade fixture is an installed item that the tenant can take with them when they end their lease.

9. a. Scarcity is an economic characteristic of land.

10. b. Accretion is the addition of land when sand or soil is naturally deposited from rivers, streams or lakes.

11. c. Permission was granted for a specified period of time.

12. b. A suit for specific performance, often times, is when there is a defaulting party. In this case the non-defaulting party is suing to force the defaulting party to carry out the terms of the contract.

13. a. Reasons to discharge a contract include: operation of law, impossibility of performance, mutual agreement of the parties to cancel, substantial performance, partial performance.

14. d. At this point the broker has a signed offer to present to the seller.

15. b. Novation occurs when the lender substitutes a new obligation for an old one.

16. c. A listing is an employment contract in which the broker provides professional services to the client.

17. a. Both the exclusive-agency and the exclusive-right-to-sell listings have only one broker.

18. c. Since the broker performed his duties she owes him their commission.

19. b. Highest and best use is the most probable use to which a property is used or suited that results in its "highest value."

20. a. Original purchase price is not compared when using the sales comparison approach.

21. d. PITI stands for principal, interest, taxes and insurance

22. b. In a fixed rate loan, the interest rate stays the same for the duration of the loan.

23. c. Gross Income Multiplier = sales price/annual gross income

24. c. When a property is pledged for a loan without giving up possession this is known as hypothecation.

25. d. An appraiser is an individual who is qualified by training, education and experience to estimate value.

26. b. Common area assessments are also known as homeowner association dues.

27. b. Eviction is when a tenant is legally expelled from the property.

28. c. A recorder is a county clerk, who collects fees for documents filed as well as maintains public real property records.

29. a. A 1003 is the loan application form that be used by lenders.

30. d. In a Veterans Administration (VA) loan transaction, once the appraisal is done the VA issues a Certificate of Reasonable Value.

31. c. Fannie Mae and Freddie Mac are government sponsored entities that were chartered by Congress.

32. b. Regulation Z gives most borrowers three days to rescind the transaction.

33. d. 403(b) and 401(k) are employer-sponsored investment plans.

34. a. Conventional loan amounts below $417,000 are conforming.

35. d. FACTA was designed to enhance the accuracy of borrower financial information, fight identity theft, and expand consumer access to credit.

36. c. Mortgage insurance is required when the LTV is greater than 80%.

37. c. Economic obsolescence is when a property loses value due to surrounding factors such as environmental and social forces.

38. a. The conveyance will be valid as his age at that time will be 19.

39. a. Listing agreements must have a "from and to" date.

40. b. An acknowledgment is a formal declaration before a public official such as a notary public.

41. c. Involuntary alienation transfers are generally carried out by operation of law.

42. d. A note is a legal document requiring a borrower to repay a mortgage loan during a specified period of time at a stated interest rate.

43. b. A leaseback is when a seller conveys the property to a buyer and the seller leases the property back from the buyer.

44. a. A trustee is a fiduciary who controls property for the benefit of another person.

45. c. A fee simple is an unconditional unlimited estate of inheritance.

46. d. Time and date of recording establish priority.

47. b. Constructive notice is based on the legal presumption that an individual may obtain information by diligent inquiry.

48. c. A purchase money transaction is the acquisition of real estate.

49. a. Property sales price results in a credit to the seller and a debit to the buyer.

50. b. The buyer should receive the security deposit credit once the deed is transferred to them.

51. b. Utility companies i.e., those companies that own the equipment are generally granted an easement as they have a right to enter and work on the property.

52. a. An easement by necessity is an easement granted by law and court action that is necessary for full enjoyment of the land.

53. c. The Virginia purchase and sale agreement states that the seller must maintain insurance on the home. The purchaser can terminate the contract or he can accept the damaged property and an assignment of the proceeds from the insurance company.

54. a. The law goes back to the English common law.

55. b. Contract for deed, also known as a land contract, is when the buyer pays installments to the seller for a specified period of time, but the seller retains title to the property during that period.

56. d. A net listing is based on the net price the seller will receive if the property is sold.

57. d. Cost is the original capital outlay for labor, land, profit and materials.

58. c. A will takes effect upon the death of the decedent.

59. b. In a condominium the owner owns the airspace in their unit

60. d. A rate and term refinance puts no funds into the borrower's hands .

61. b. The secondary market is where "pools" of existing mortgages are bought and sold.

62. a. The seller must pay off and/or remove any liens before the title can be delivered free and clear.

63. c. The principal amount is the buyer's credit as this is what will the buyer will have to pay.

64. a. The lender will order an appraisal which will be done by an appraiser, someone who has been trained and educated and is experienced in estimating value.

65. d. A public official who establishes the value for tax purposes is an assessor.

66. c. Month-to-month tenancy renews itself at each expiration.

67. d. A lease does not need to be recorded.

68. a. Money set aside for the replacement of common property in a condominium or cooperative project is called a replacement reserve fund.

69. b. Corrective maintenance involves the actual repair of the building's equipment.

70. c. Zoning is a tool for implementing a local plan to prevent incompatible land uses.

71. b. A *lis pendens* is a legal notice that a legal suit has been filed which could affect the property.

72. a. Per RESPA, kickbacks are illegal.

73. d. A unilateral contract is when a promise is exchanged for performance.

74. c. The GLBA falls under the jurisdiction of the Federal Trade Commission.

75. a. A fixed rate loan is structured for the repayment of borrowed funds.

76. a. A mortgage banker is a firm that can originate, sell and service mortgage loans.

77. d. A vacancy rate lower than 5% generally indicates that rents are too low.

78. c. Improvements can reach a point in which they no longer add value but rather diminish the returns.

79. a. Under FIRREA, appraisers need to be licensed by the state in order to appraise real property valued over $1,000,000 in federally related transactions.

80. d. Under Virginia general law, brokers do not have to disclose if a suicide or homicide occur in a home.

81. d. Confidentiality is an agent responsibility.

82. b. Reconciliation is the art of weighing the findings and analyzing from three approaches to value.

83. c. Negative cash flow can be offset by an increase in property value.

84. a. Chapter 13 bankruptcy has an automatic stay provision.

85. b. HOA dues in Virginia take precedence over other liens and the HOA can take the homeowner to court and even force a sale.

86. d. Take $225,000 - $80,000 = $145,000 to get the increased value. Then take increased value/ purchased price. $145,000/$80,000 = 1.8. You can find the annual appreciation rate by 1.8/20 years = 9%.

87. c. Under Virginia law as long as the borrower has met lender requirements and the commitment letter has correct wording, it is a binding agreement.

88. a. In Virginia sellers do not have to sign the seller's statement of property condition, but they must disclose known defects if asked.

89. b. The Virginia Circuit Breaker Tax Credit deals with property tax credits for seniors over 65 who qualify.

90. a. The Spite Fence Law says that a fence that unnecessarily exceeds 6 feet in height and is maliciously erected for the purpose of annoying the neighbors may be deemed a private nuisance.

91. d. Tenancy by the entirety is when an ownership arises between a husband and wife and a single instrument transfers property to both of them which says nothing about the type of ownership.

92. b. Unpaid liens are generally found in a title search.

93. a. In Virginia the fee to record the discharge of a mortgage is currently $75.00.

94. c. The earnest money deposit is not a condition of an offer to purchase a home. It lets the seller know the buyer is serious about purchasing the home.

95. c. Severalty means that all others have been severed or cut off.

96. c. The words of conveyance can be found in the granting clause.

97. d. Because traffic is limited, the shopping center will have the greatest risk and therefore the highest cap rate.

98. b. Open listings are also known as nonexclusive agreements

99. a. With an exculpatory clause in place the buyer is not responsible for the debt because it acts as a non-recourse loan.

100. c. General warranty deeds contain covenants that warrant the new owner's clear and undisturbed title.

Made in the USA
Lexington, KY
06 June 2016